Allyn and Bacon

Quick Guide to the Internet for Composition

1998 Edition

H. Eric Branscomb

Salem State College

Allyn and Bacon
Boston • London • Toronto • Sydney • Tokyo • Singapore

Macintosh is a registered trademark of Apple Computer, Inc.

Microsoft is a registered trademark of Microsoft Corporation. Windows, Windows95, and Microsoft Internet Explorer are trademarks of Microsoft Corporation.

Netscape Navigator and the Netscape Navigator logo are registered trademarks of Netscape Communications Corporation

Sprint is a registered trademark of Sprint Communications Company L.P. Sprint Internet Passport is a service mark of Sprint Communications Company L.P.

ISBN 0-205-27981-3

Printed in the United States of America

10   9   8   7   6   5   4   3   01   00   99   98

Contents

Get Connected Now!

Load, click and cruise on the Internet with Sprint Internet Passport (SM) for news, information, entertainment and much more. With Sprint Internet Passport, you get full-service, direct Internet access from Sprint, friendly customer service support on-line or by phone 24 hours a day, seven days a week. You'll be able to easily browse around the World Wide Web, and you'll also receive one E-mail account for communicating with family, friends and colleagues. In addition when you get connected with Sprint Internet Passport, you'll receive full access to more than 18,000 Usenet newsgroups, local service from more than 200 U.S. cities (more planned in 1997) and reliable service from one of the Internet's largest carriers.

Pricing for Sprint Internet Passport is $19.95 a month for unlimited use,* or you can pay only for the hours you use at a rate of $1.50 per hour. For your convenience, we'll bill your VISA®, MasterCard® or American Express®.

Just double click on the Sprint icon to start your Internet experience.

Sprint Installation Instructions

DO NOT INSTALL SOFTWARE until you have read the Software License agreement which appears on the CD.

If you currently use Netscape® Navigator as your Internet browser, Sprint Internet Passport will automatically overwrite that software. However, with just a little extra care and effort, Sprint Internet Passport will nicely coexist on your system with your current software. More information and details on the exact steps necessary to preserve your current configuration can be found at http://www.sprint.com/passport, or you can call us at 1-800-786-1400.

*Nation-wide 800 Access Number includes surcharge of $4.80 per hour if local service is not available in your area.

Windows® 3.1 Users

1. Insert the *Sprint Internet Passport* installation CD into your CD-ROM drive.

2. In *Program Manager* or *File Manager,* select *File* from the menu bar, and then select Run.

3. In the *Command Line* field, type *D:\INSTALL* (where D: represents the drive letter of your CD-ROM).

4. Click *OK,* then follow the on-screen prompts to complete the software setup. When you're prompted to do so, allow setup to restart Windows®.

5. When restart is complete, double-click on the *Sprint Internet Passport Account Setup* icon in the *Sprint Internet Passport* program group.

6. Follow the on-screen prompts to set up your *Sprint Internet Passport* account.

7. When registration is completed, double-click on the *Sprint Internet Passport* icon in the *Sprint Internet Passport* program group.

8. Click *Dial.*

You're ready to begin!

Windows95® Users

1. If you have never been on-line before, be sure to have your Windows95® diskettes or *Sprint Internet Passport* CD handy.

2. Insert the *Sprint Internet Passport* installation CD into your CD-ROM drive. On most systems, the setup process will begin automatically within about 10 seconds.

3. If the setup program doesn't begin automatically, click the *Start* button on your Task Bar and then click *Run.* In the *Run* window, type

D:\INSTALL (where *D:* represents the drive letter of your CD-ROM) and click *OK*.

4. Follow the on-screen prompts to complete the software setup. If you're prompted for a Windows95® diskette, place the required diskette in *Drive A:;* if you're prompted for the Windows95® CD, remove the *Sprint Internet Passport* CD from your CD-ROM drive and insert your Windows95® CD. If you're prompted to do so, allow set up to restart your computer.

5. Double-click the *Sprint Internet Passport Account Setup* icon in the *Navigator* window.

6. Follow the on-screen prompts to set up your Sprint Internet Passport account.

7. Once registration is completed, double-click on the *Dial Sprint Internet Passport* icon on your desktop to connect to Sprint Internet Services.

8. If the password field is blank (no stars), enter your password.

9. Click Connect.

10. Double-click the *Sprint Internet Passport* icon on your desktop to launch the Sprint Internet Passport Browser (Netscape Navigator).

You're ready to begin!

Macintosh Users

1. Insert the Sprint Internet Passport installation CD into your CD-ROM drive.

2. The *Sprint Internet Passport* window will appear on your desktop. Inside this window, double-click the *Installer* icon.

3. Follow the on-screen prompts to complete the software setup. Be sure to take the default settings. (Note that default settings are outlined in black on your screen.)

4. When setup is complete, you will be prompted to restart your computer. Click on *Restart*.

5. When restart is complete, the Account Setup window appears. Click on the *Next* arrow in the Account Setup window.

6. Follow the on-screen prompts to set up your Sprint Internet Passport account.

   During Account Setup, your computer will attempt to connect to the registration service to open your account. *If you are using Macintosh System 7.1,* you will be prompted to restart your computer. Click on Restart. When restart is complete, the Account Setup window appears. Click on the *Connect Now* arrow to continue with Account Setup.

7. When registration is complete, you will be prompted to restart your computer. Click on *Restart.*

8. When restart is complete, double-click on the *Sprint Internet Passport* icon in the Sprint Internet Passport window. *FreePPP* will connect you to Sprint Internet Services, and the Sprint Internet Passport browser will launch.

You're ready to begin!

Exiting your Sprint Internet Passport Account

If you're using Windows® 3.1

- Close *Sprint Internet Passport (Netscape Navigator)* by clicking on *File* and then clicking on *Exit.*

- Close any other open Internet client applications (e.g., IRC, FTP, and Telnet sessions).

- Disconnect from *Sprint Internet Passport* by clicking the *Disconnect* button in the *Sprint Internet Dialer* box.

If you're using Windows95®

- Close *Sprint Internet Passport (Netscape Navigator)* by clicking on *File* and then clicking on *Exit.*

- A message will come up stating that there are open modem connections. Choose "yes" to disconnect from the Internet.

- Close any other open Internet client applications (e.g., IRC, FTP, and Telnet sessions).
- Check to make sure there is no button on the Task Bar labeled *Connected to Sprint Internet.* If there is, click on it to bring up the *Sprint Dialer Dialogue* box and click on the *Disconnect* button.

If you're using a Macintosh

- Close *Sprint Internet Passport (Netscape Navigator).*
- Double-click on the *FreePPP Setup* icon in the *Sprint Internet Passport* folder.
- Click *Disconnect.*

Notes

Be sure to record your:

- Dial Access Number
- Sprint Internet Passport Password
- E-mail Address
- Sprint Internet Passport Log-in ID

A README file has been included on your Sprint Internet Passport CD. Windows® 3.X users can find it here: *D:\WIN.31\DISK5\README.TXT* (where D: represents your CD-ROM drive). Windows95® users can access the file by clicking on *Start,* clicking on *Run,* typing *D:\WIN.95\DISK5\README.TXT* (where D: represents your CD-ROM drive), and clicking *OK.*

For Macintosh users, the *README.txt File* can be found in the Sprint Internet window on the CD.

Your software will automatically search for and attempt to identify your modem. However, if setup encounters difficulties, you may need to identify your modem manually. See the *README.txt File* for more information. Be sure to verify your pricing plan selection.

Be sure your registration address matches your credit card billing address. If your credit card company uses ZIP+4, it is important that you include the extra 4 digits.

If you live in an area where local calls can span two or more area codes, you may want to modify the 1+Area Code settings in your dialer. See the *README.txt File* for more information.

Please review all the numbers available to help ensure your modem dialer is set for a local call. If you are unsure if a number is a local call, check with your local telephone company. Please note that in some areas, a call may be considered long distance, even though it does not require dialing a "1" or "0".

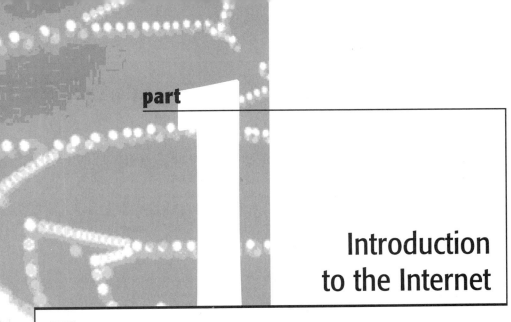

part 1

Introduction to the Internet

The Internet—Communication in the '90s

The Internet is a loose affiliation of computers and computer networks. These networks range in size from small, one-computer operations of individual users and small businesses and to the super-sized networks at large corporations and universities.

Who's in Charge Here?

You can think of the Internet as a kind of United Nations, serving only to facilitate the rules by which information is passed from one member to another. The Internet is nothing more than a few committees who establish the rules and languages by which the computers in the member networks talk to each other. Just as the United Nations does not control what goes on within the member countries, there is no organization called the "Internet" that controls what goes on inside each member network.

The Internet is also international in scope and no single government controls it. On one hand this near anarchy has allowed the Internet to grow at an unbelievable rate, but on the other hand the lack of a governing body means that the Internet is a bit like the old Wild West— anything and everything goes, and there's no sheriff to keep law and order.

The Information Explosion

The Internet has been a boon to college students, and nowhere will this be more evident than in your composition classes. Thanks to computer network technology, you may be able to do all your research without leaving your room, write and submit your papers without using any paper, ask your teacher a question when she's a thousand miles away, and engage in conversations with other students or experts in a field when you're alone. Although not every student has access to this technology, these dreams from a decade ago are now a reality for many.

The Internet has intensified and accelerated the production and dissemination of information—in computerese, the input, output, and throughput have increased dramatically. There is exponentially more information and misinformation available; it's available more quickly and easily than ever before in the history of humankind. But the rules of dealing with this information have changed. Twenty years ago a major task of a student writing a research paper was finding information; today it's avoiding being overwhelmed by too much information too rapidly.

In addition to overwhelming you with sheer quantities of information, the Internet has the potential to mislead you with biased, slanted, or simply wrong information. Your challenge, as a writing student heading into the twenty-first century, is more than ever to be able to separate fact from fiction, truth from half-truths and lies, valid and reliable information from propaganda. In the era of printed information, there was always someone—an editor, a reputable publishing company, a panel of experts—to decide what was worthy of publication and what wasn't. They acted as filters for you, helping to block much bad information before it ever saw the light of day. No more. You have to do it yourself.

In order to access this new endless universe of information, you need to learn new skills. When all you have is your library's card catalog and a copy of *The Reader's Guide to Periodical Literature,* finding a limited amount of information is not difficult. But imagine if you opened a drawer in the card catalog and looked under a particular heading and found two million listings! You need to learn how to manipulate the strange new tools—the so-called "search engines"—the Internet provides for you.

There really has been an information explosion all around you, but you must be sure not to be blown away by it.

part

1

Significance for Communication, Education, and Research

The Internet has been compared to a large worldwide library, but it's more than that. It's been compared to a communication medium like the telephone, but it's more than that as well. And it's been compared to a giant democratic publishing company that publishes everything it receives, rejecting no one. As a student, you will be able to make use of all three of these capabilities of the Internet.

For college composition classes, you will very likely be writing a variety of papers: perhaps some personal narrative, analyses of literature, persuasion pieces, and maybe a research paper or two. The actual subject matter of your writing will vary widely, so that in some sense you will have to become a master of knowledge of a number of different fields.

If you have a research paper to write, for example, your college's library catalog may be on-line (though the actual books and journals, for the most part, are not), along with the other resources and databases your library makes available to its patrons. If your library offers you First Search or Lexis-Nexis, say, you will be able to access those sources right from your own computer, without needing to trudge down to the library itself and wait for a computer terminal to open up.

The World Wide Web has become an unimaginably large source of information, and as long as you keep your critical guard up at all times, you will find it a relatively quick and easy reference source. In literally just a few seconds at your computer, you can have at your fingertips two million or more potentially relevant sources of information. You can check a fact quickly (just how many grams of fat *are* in a Big Mac, anyway?) or read complete reports of research or government documents (regardless of what you hear on the news, what did the Oakland School Board *really* say in its Ebonics proposal? The actual text is on-line.).

To deepen your interest and to help you think of more ideas and arguments and insights, you can listen to (and even participate in) any number of the tens of thousands of electronic discussions occurring worldwide over the Internet. In these topically-arranged listservs and Usenet newsgroups, everyone from the most respected experts to the least knowledgeable beginners and outsiders has the opportunity to add in their $.02's worth (or, in non-Internet-speak, two cents' worth).

As you begin to organize and compose your paper, you may want to discuss some issues of either your subject matter or the actual composing process. You can E-mail some concerns to a friend or other trusted person, someone you know who will give you good advice. It may be someone else in your class or a friend from home who's now at a different college. Many of your instructors will allow you to electronically submit rough drafts of your papers early for some feedback on your ideas and your information before the paper is actually due for a grade.

Person-To-Person: Using E-mail

Electronic mail, or E-mail, is one of the most important applications of the Internet. E-mail is personal correspondence between individual users, and is the electronic equivalent to the familiar paper-based postal service.

How It Works

Every Internet Service Provider operates a post office 24 hours a day, 365 days per year to receive messages sent to its customers and to forward the mail they send to other people. Messages addressed to you are stored on the post office computer until you are ready to read them.

When you send an E-mail message to another person, you first transmit the message to your provider's post office which starts the message on its way to the post office at the recipient's service provider. Messages are usually passed between several post office computers on their way from one provider to another.

Personal Addresses on the Internet Each user on the Internet has a unique name. The name is made up of two parts: the user name and the domain name. The user name identifies the individual user, and the domain name identifies the Internet Service Provider.

For example, the E-mail address "psmith@uiuc.edu" is for a user named "P. Smith" at an organization (domain) called "uiuc.edu". The two pieces are always separated by '@'.

All domain names for organizations in the United States end with a three-letter abbreviation which specifies the type of organization. The common abbreviations are:

- .com   a company or business
- .edu   an educational institution
- .net   a commercial Internet service provider
- .org   an organization that is not a business

part

1

Domain names from other parts of the world end with a two-letter abbreviation which specifies the country in which the organization is located. For example, "pat_smith@emwac.ed.ac.uk" is for a user named "Pat Smith" at an organization located in the United Kingdom.

Mail Programs

There are many different mail programs available, and they all provide similar functions and use similar terminology. We're going to give example from two popular mail programs: Netscape Mail and Microsoft Internet Mail.

Mail programs organize your messages in areas called *folders*. Typical folders are called Inbox, which holds the mail that has been sent to you, **Outbox** which holds mail you have written but not yet sent, and **Sent** which hold copies of messages you have sent to other people. You can also create your own folders as a way to save messages you have received in an organized fashion.

part

1

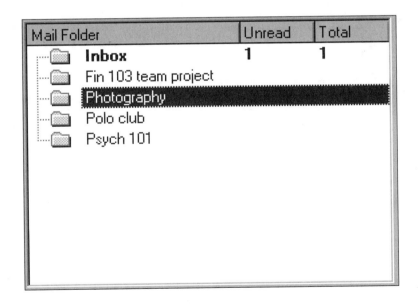

Mail Folder	Unread	Total
Inbox	1	1
Fin 103 team project		
Photography		
Polo club		
Psych 101		

Using folders to organize messages you have received or sent can be a very convenient way to maintain a complete record of an E-mail "conversation."

Sending a Message

In this section we'll go step-by-step through the process of sending an E-mail message to another user. The steps are given for the Netscape Mail and Microsoft Internet Mail programs. If you are using a different mail program consult the program's documentation for complete instructions.

Using Netscape Mail

1. Click the To:Mail button in the toolbar or select the **New Mail Message** option from the **File** menu.

part
1

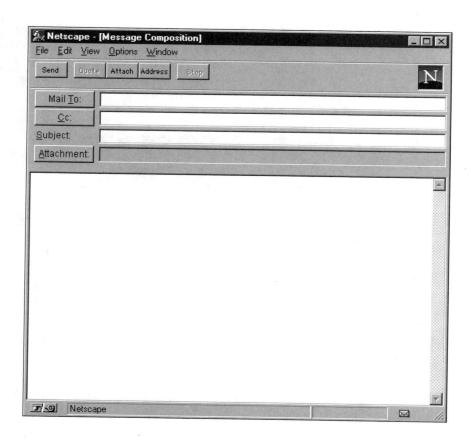

2. Type the recipient's E-mail address on the "Mail To:" line. If you want to send the same message to more than one person, put a semicolon between the E-mail names. You can build up an electronic address book which can be accessed by clicking on the **Mail To:** button.

3. Press TAB to move to the "CC:" line. Type the address of people to whom you would like to send a copy of the message. Don't type anything here if you don't want to send copies or you have already listed everyone on the "To:" line.

4. Press TAB again and type a subject line for the message.

5. Press TAB again and type the body of your message. When you have finished writing the message, either click the **Send** button or choose the **Send Now** option from the **File** menu.

Using Microsoft Internet Mail

1. Click the **New Message** button in the toolbar or select the **New Message** option from the **Mail** menu.

2. Type the recipient's E-mail address on the "To:" line. If you want to send the same message to more than one person, put a semicolon between the E-mail names. You can build up an electronic address book which can be accessed by clicking on the file card icon.

3. Press TAB to move to the "CC:" line. Type the address of people to whom you would like to send a copy of the message. Don't type anything here if you don't want to send copies or you have already listed everyone on the "To:" line.

4. Press TAB again and type a subject line for the message.

5. Press TAB again and type the body of your message. When you have finished writing the message, either click the send icon or choose the **Send Message** option from the **File** menu.

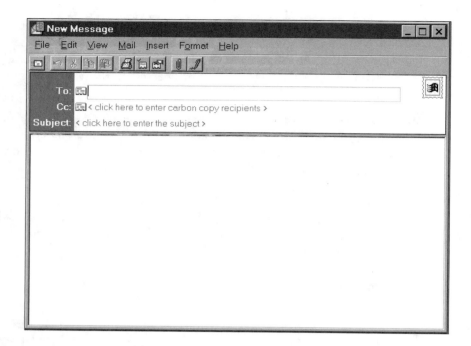

Your E-mail message starts it journey to the recipient's system as soon as you press the Send key. Once you send a message there is no way to get it back or stop it from reaching its destination.

Now practice sending a message by sending a message to yourself. Start your mail program and follow the steps listed above.

- Type your own E-mail address in the "Mail To:" or "To:" field.
- Leave the "CC:" field blank.
- Type "Test Message" on the "Subject line"
- Type "This is a test message. Did you get it?" for the body of the message. When you're finished use the "Send" option to send the message to yourself.

Reading and Responding to Messages

Using Netscape Mail

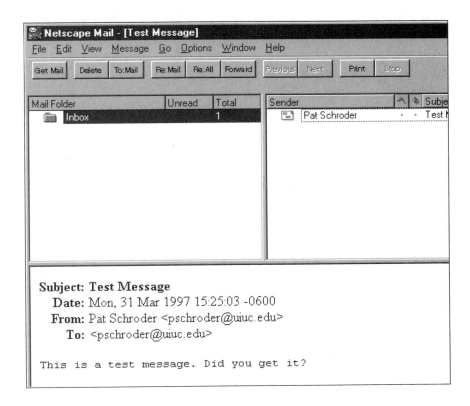

1. When you start Netscape Mail, the display shows a list of messages that have been sent to you. Messages that you have not yet read are listed in bold type.

   The "Sender" column shows who send the message, the "Subject" column displays the subject line, and the "Date" column shows the date on which the message was received.

2. The message you just sent to yourself should be listed in the window. Double-click the message line in the listing.

3. The message appears in the lower part of the window.

part

1

Using Microsoft Internet Mail

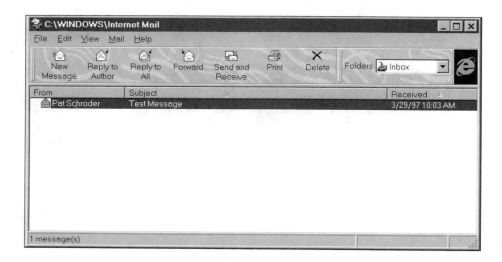

1. When you start Microsoft Internet Mail, the display shows a list of messages that have been sent to you. Messages that you have not yet read are listed in bold type.

   The "From" column shows who send the message, the "Subject" column displays the subject line, and the "Received" column shows the date on which the message was received.

2. The message you just sent to yourself should be listed in the window. Double-click the message line in the listing to open the mail reading window.

3. The message reader pops open and shows you the message.

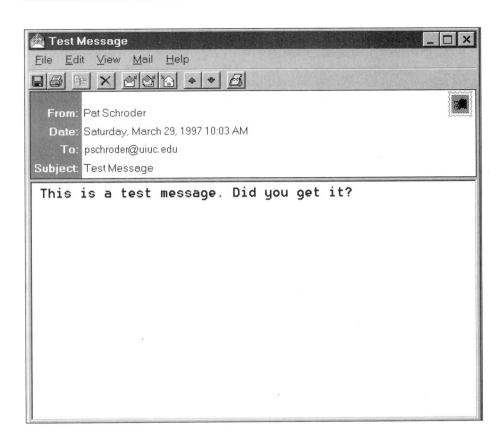

After you've read the message you can reply to it, then you can either delete it or file it in a folder for later reference. Using the reply feature of your mail reader is how you carry on an E-mail conversation. You receive a message that you reply to, then you receive a reply to your reply, you reply to that, and so on.

This kind of E-mail conversation may take place over a period of a few days or weeks; it's sometimes hard to keep the context of the conversation in mind when reading replies. Mail reader programs include a feature called Quoting that copies the message you are replying to and makes it part of your reply. When you use this feature you send back the original message along with your reply. This helps the person reading the reply remember the context of the message.

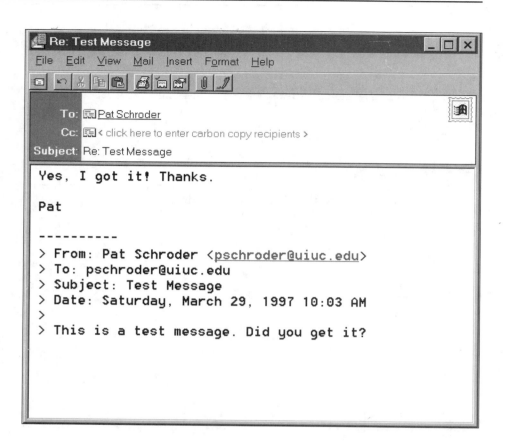

part
1

How to Locate Addresses

One major problem with the Internet is that there is no equivalent of the phone book. If you don't know someone's E-mail address there is no way to look them up in a directory. There are a few experimental directory assistance services in development, but so far they cover only a very small fraction of the millions of people who have E-mail addresses.

As you work with the Internet you will find many opportunities to compile an address book of E-mail addresses for future reference. Build up your own address book by watching for addresses on paper-based and electronic documents. Look for addresses on letterheads and other stationary. You should also copy the E-mail addresses from messages you receive. When you start surfing the Web (covered in a later chapter), you will have more opportunities to discover E-mail addresses.

Until your address book is built up adequately, or if you're really desperate for an E-mail address, you might try some of the available E-mail searches. Don't get your hopes up, however; you have far less than a 50/50 chance of finding what you're looking for. For a complete discussion and set of tips for locating an address, try the Web site *FAQ: How to Find People's E-mail Addresses* <http://www.cis.ohio-state.edu/hypertext/faq/usenet/finding-addresses/faq.html>. But the best resources, inadequate as they may be, are the following:

- Bigfoot <http://www.bigfoot.com>
- WhoWhere <http://www.whowhere.com/>
- Four11 <http://www.four11.com/>
- Internet Address Finder <http://www.iaf.net/>
- Switchboard <http://www.switchboard.com/>
- Phonebooke [sic] <http://www.phonebooke.com/>
- Usenet Addresses Database <http://usenet-addresses.mit.edu/>
- Lycos EmailFind <http://www.lycos.com/emailfind.html>
- World Email Directory <http://www.worldemail.com/>

part

1

(Both *Yahoo!* and *Infoseek* offer searches of E-mail addresses from their main search pages, but both actually use the Four11 service, so they have nothing additional to offer.)

Ironically, the best way to find someone's E-mail address is simply to ask, and then add it to your address book.

E-mail Etiquette

A set of etiquette rules have been developed over the years to make electronic interactions more pleasant and orderly. You should follow these rules of behavior, sometimes called "netiquette", when using E-mail.

Don't use all upper case. Using upper case letters to emphasize words in your messages is the E-mail equivalent of shouting. It's considered very bad manners to write messages in upper case.

Use emoticons and acronyms. The person reading your messages does not have the benefit of seeing your facial expressions and body language as with a face-to-face encounter. This is a very important limitation of E-mail, and you must always consider how your words might be interpreted. It's very hard for someone to know if you are kidding or are being very serious. *Emoticons* and acronyms have been developed over the years as a way of showing facial expressions or conveying feelings in the text of a message.

An emoticon is a set of characters that represent an emotion or facial expression. Common emoticons you may see in messages are:

:-)	smile
;-)	wink
:-(	frown
<g>	grin
<vbg>	very big grin

An acronym is a form of shorthand. The letters of the acronym stand for an expression. Common acronyms in messages are:

part
1

AFAIK	as far as I know
IMO	in my opinion
IMHO	in my humble opinion
BTW	by the way
OTOH	on the other hand
CU	see you

Use emoticons and acronyms in your messages to help convey the subtle (or not-so-subtle) meanings behind your words. It may make a world of difference whether you write "Idiot!<g>" or "Idiot!" to the person reading your message.

Don't quote everything. Although quoting is a convenient way to maintain the context of a series of messages, messages become unreadable if you quote too much or quote a quote that includes a quote. Quote judiciously.

Keep your signature short. Some mail programs allow you to set up a *signature block*. This is a few lines of information that acts as your signature on a mail message. It's best not to put too much information in your signature block; your name and organizational affiliation are enough. You should not put your postal mailing address, phone number, fax number, web site address, and favorite quote in your signature. Signatures should be very short, not longer than the messages they are attached to. Some people pay for E-mail services or have slow connections to the Internet, and this unnecessary information costs them time and money.

Be polite. Somewhere a researcher is studying the curious phenomenon that people will write things in an E-mail message that they would never say to someone's face. On the Internet, being intentionally rude and insulting is called *flaming* and has become a kind of sport for some people. You can unwittingly become the target of a flame attack by simply making a breach of netiquette in a public forum. If someone sends you an E-mail message calling you a "clueless newbie," you've been flamed.

Many people enjoy flaming newcomers to the net. They will try to insult you because of your lack of experience using the net or the incorrect use of Internet terminology. Resist the temptation to reply to a flame attack. A flaming reply to a flame starts what is called a *flame war,* a kind of pointless Internet shouting match that can go on and on forever until one of the participants finally gives in at which point the opponent has "won" the war.

It's one thing to point out a mistake in someone's message, but do it in a polite way and back up your point with facts. A critical response should be more like a debate than a brawl. Don't just send a message saying, "Everyone knows such-and-such, and only a complete idiot and fool would think otherwise." Life's short. Lighten up.

You can't take it back. While no one has the time (and very few people the inclination) to go snooping into other people's E-mail, you should remember that the Internet is not a secure medium. Don't write anything—even in a private E-mail—that you wouldn't want posted on a bulletin board in your student union. Messages can be intercepted and read; your school or ISP archives all E-mail sent through its system and can produce it by court order; you will regret angry or mean-spirited messages in the morning. Think before you hit the "send" button. Once you've sent it, you can't take it back.

part

1

On-Line Discussions: Newsgroups and Listservers

Newsgroups vs. E-mail

E-mail is a great person-to-person communication medium, but it's not very good for large group interaction. If the group consists of more than a few people, adding all the names to the "To:" or "CC:" list gets to be a tedious chore and it's hard to be sure that everyone sees the all of the replies. *Newsgroups* were developed to address this limitation.

A newsgroup is an electronic message board. The message board keeps track of several discussions simultaneously by organizing the messages and replies in groups called *threads*. A thread starts with the original message, or *post,* and includes all of the replies made by every participant in the discussion. You can follow the discussion by reading the thread from beginning to end. This makes it possible for several people to collaborate on a project or continue a discussion over a long period of time.

part

1

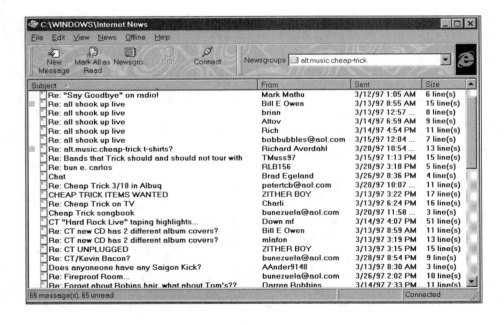

A program called a news reader is used to read newsgroups and follow the threads. News readers operate very much like E-mail programs, but they also provide features that let you follow threads and keep track of your place in several continuing discussions. We'll be looking at the Netscape Navigator News Reader and the Microsoft Internet News programs for examples in this section. Other news readers offer similar services and work in much the same way.

Locating Newsgroups

part

1

You can participate in tens of thousands of public and private newsgroups. You are usually invited to join a private newsgroup or find out about it because of your affiliation in an organization or participation in an activity. The discussion topics in a private newsgroup are likely to be very focused.

Your Internet Service Provider will carry as many as 20,000 public newsgroups in which you can participate. Just about every topic you can think of is covered, and a few that may shock and possibly offend you as well. When you hear stories on the news about all the smut and terrible things that are available on the Internet, the reporters are usually talking about newsgroups.

Newsgroups are organized in a hierarchy. There are a small number of main categories, each of which is broken down into subtopics, and further broken down into specific topics of interest. A sampling of the main categories you are likely to encounter includes:

comp	computer science and general computer-related topics
news	newsgroups pertaining to the operation of the Internet newsgroup system
rec	hobbies, recreational activities, and various arts
sci	scientific research, the applications of science and engineering, and some social sciences
soc	social issues
misc	anything that doesn't fit into the above categories
alt	"alternative" newsgroups, many unusual topics

part
1

The subtopics are, of course, different for each of the main categories. For example, within the "rec" category there is a subtopic "photo" for photographic-related discussions. This group of topics is called the "rec.photo" newsgroups. Notice that the main category is named first, followed by a period, then the subtopic name. The specific newsgroup dedicated to the discussion of photographing people is called "rec.photo.people".

In college composition courses, you really are not limited in the kinds of subject matter you may be writing about, so conceivably any number of the 20,000 or so newsgroups may be of interest to you at some time or another in your career. A useful and fairly complete searchable index of newsgroups is available on the Web at <http://www.tile.net/tile/news/index.html>. More specifically relevant, there is a smattering of groups devoted to various aspects of composition and writing, and though they are frequented mostly by professionals, you may want to lurk for a while yourself.

- alt.books.stephen-king
- alt.education.email-project
- alt.horror.creative
- alt.journalism.criticism
- alt.journalism.newspapers
- alt.lesbian.feminist.poetry
- alt.literacy.adult
- alt.usage.english
- alt.uu.announce
- bit.listserv.dorothyl
- bit.listserv.literary
- bit.listserv.techwr-l
- bit.listserv.words-l
- humanities.lit.authors.shakespeare
- misc.writing
- rec.arts.poems
- sci.research

part

1

The list of newsgroups available to you is downloaded to your computer and kept up to date by the news group reader program. Specific instructions for browsing the newsgroup list depend on the particular newsgroup reader program.

Netscape Navigator News Reader

1. Select the **Show All Newsgroups** from the **Options** menu of Netscape Navigator. The list of available newsgroups is shown in the **News Servers** window. This window is organized like an outline. To locate a newsgroup you have to "expand" the levels of the outline. Click on the '+' sign next to an entry to see the subentries. Keep on

clicking '+' signs until you get to the lowest level in the section you are interested in.

part

1

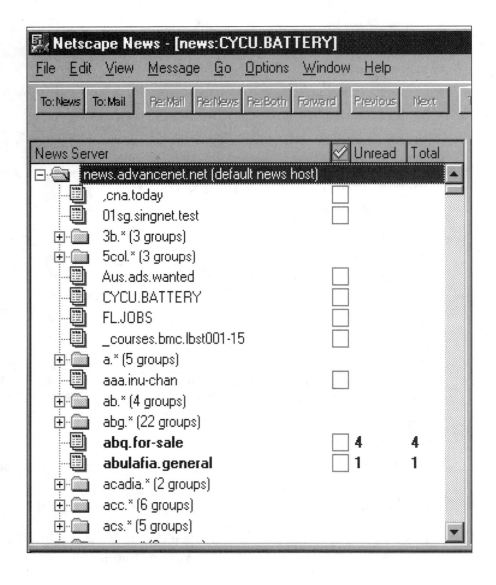

2. Click on the newsgroup name in the Newsgroups box. A list of messages appears in the window.

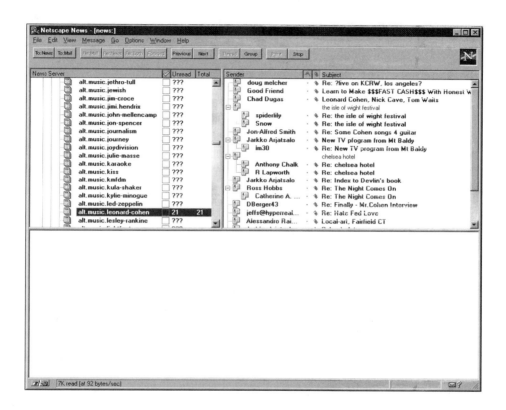

Microsoft Internet News

1. Click the **Newsgroups** button in the toolbar or select the **Newsgroups** option from the **News** menu.

2. Click the **All** tab in the newsgroups window to display the entire list of newsgroups. You can browse the entire list of newsgroups by scrolling the list, or locate a newsgroup by typing a word in the "Display newsgroups which contain" box at the top of the page.

3. Click on the newsgroup name in the Newsgroups box and then click the **Go To** button to immediately see the messages for that newsgroup.

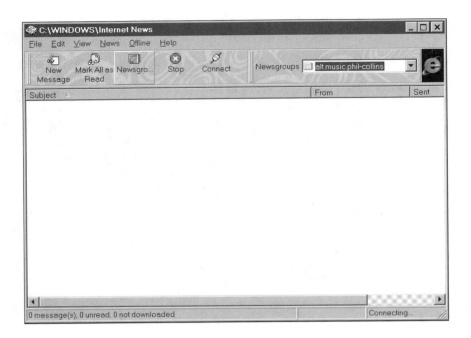

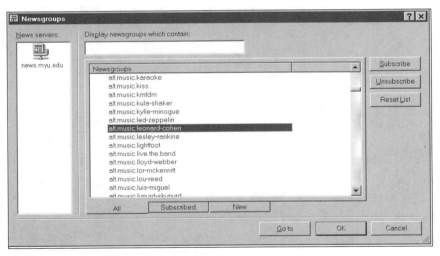

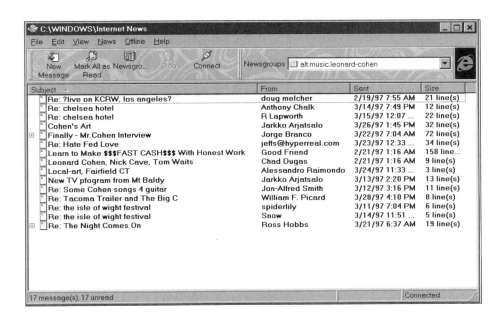

Reading Messages

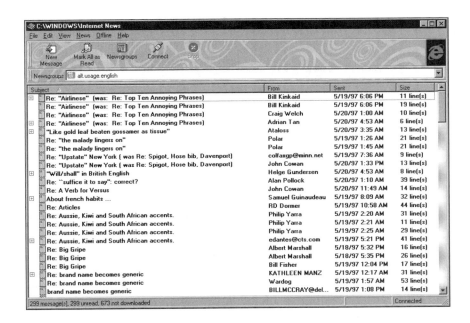

Once you have selected a newsgroup the news reader program displays a list of messages. The title of the message, name of the sender, and the date on which the message was written are displayed. You will often see "Re:" as the first part of the message title. That means "Regarding" and indicates that the message is a reply to a previous message on the same topic. Some news reader software automatically groups the messages by topic. A series of messages on the same topic is called a *thread*.

Double click on the message title line to display the message. The text of the message is displayed in a window.

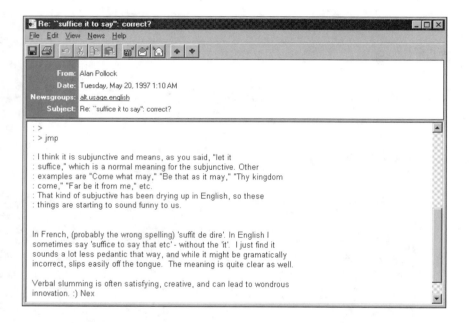

Once you locate a newsgroup that you are interested in reading, you have two choices. You can subscribe to the newsgroup and let your news reader program keep track of which messages you have already seen, or you can just drop in from time to time and notice whether there are new messages. Subscribing doesn't cost you anything and is the most convenient option of you are going to be a frequent reader of a particular newsgroup.

Subscribing is easy. If you use Microsoft Internet News, simply click the **Subscribe** button after selecting the newsgroup in the newsgroup window. If you use Netscape Navigator News Reader, click the checkbox next to the newsgroup name in the **News Server** window.

Posting and Responding to Messages

It's always a good idea to follow a newsgroup for a while before posting messages yourself. Reading messages and never posting is called *lurking*. Lurk for a few days so you will know what type of messages and topics are appropriate for the list.

Replies to messages can be posted to the newsgroup for all participants to see, or you can send a personal reply to the message author by E-mail.

You can also start a new thread by posting your own message to the newsgroup. This is very similar to sending E-mail, but instead of addressing the message to one person you post it to the list for all participants to see.

Responsible Participation: Newsgroup Etiquette

All the etiquette rules that apply to E-mail apply to newsgroups as well. Since messages in newsgroups may be read by thousands of people, however, there are a few additional rules you should keep in mind.

Keep it short. Keep your messages to newsgroups short and to the point. Many people have to pay for access to the Internet and the extra time needed to download long or off-topic messages costs them money.

Don't believe everything you read. There's no control over what's posted in most newsgroups, so you're likely to find all types of information. Some of it is profane and inflammatory, and some of it is just plain wrong. If you are easily offended you should be careful which newsgroups you read. Be careful about believing anything you read in a newsgroup, especially if it's some type of rumor or gossip. Some people make a sport out of posting outlandish rumors, or intentionally post factually incorrect information. When you read a message in a newsgroup, pay attention to the name of the author. Pretty soon you will figure out who is reliable and who isn't. Newsgroups are a great source of information and peer support, but don't believe everything you read. If you have

part

1

children, you may want to restrict their access to newsgroups. Many contain language and content that's not appropriate for children.

Be tolerant. Newsgroups are read by people all over the world, many of whom do not use English as their native language. Never flame or correct anyone's spelling or grammar, and be very tolerant of misused phrases or "broken English."

Don't send spam. Easy access to the Internet has spawned a new breed of junk mail known as *spam*. Spam is a message promising a new way to loose weight, get rich quick, or something similar. Some of these messages are chain letters, others are outright scams and hoaxes. A spam message is never about the topic of the newsgroup to which it has been posted. Don't respond to spam messages, and do not post off-topic messages like that yourself!

Keep cross posting to a minimum. *Cross posting* means that a message will be sent to more than one newsgroup simultaneously. This can be compared to running from room to room at a party and carrying on the same conversation with different groups of people. Since many people who read newsgroups follow many groups on similar topics, cross posted messages almost always reach the same audience anyway. It is very annoying to see similar, but slightly different threads in different newsgroups. Never post a message to more than two or three newsgroups, and be sure you have a very good reason for doing so.

Group Discussion via E-mail (Listservers)

Setting up a newsgroup is not an easy process, so many special interest groups use a variation of E-mail to pass messages to all of the group members. A *listserver* is a program that automatically distributes messages to all the members of the list. Once you join a list, the listserver will send you all messages via standard E-mail. You can reply to a message or start a new discussion by sending an E-mail message to the listserver program instead of sending copies of a message to each member individually.

Listservers are convenient because they insure that all members of the list see all the posted messages, including all replies between members. Some listserver programs will accumulate and combine messages into a *digest*. A digest allows the listserver to send one large message to each member on a periodic basis rather than sending many small mes-

part

1

sages all the time. For very active lists it's easier for the members and more efficient for the Internet for list members to use the digest form.

Finding a Mailing List

There are thousands of mailing lists, so how do you find lists on your favorite topics? There are several ways. First, you will see references to lists as you read newsgroups and carry on discussions with colleagues. Second, there are some resources on the World Wide Web that you can search by topic to find the names of mailing lists that may be of interest. And third, you can obtain lists of lists via E-mail.

The easiest way to find a listserv is to check one of the directories on the World Wide Web. Probably the most popular and easy to use directory is *Liszt*, available at <http://www.liszt.com>. It's searchable and provides you with simple instructions for subscribing to a list that you find interesting.

You will find once again, as with the newsgroups, that there aren't many discussion lists devoted specifically to composition as a subject. From American Literature to Women's History, the whole range of scholarly fields is open to you as you write. Another point to consider: Your instructor may very likely set up a listserv specifically for your composition class and ask that you participate in on-line discussions with your classmates.

For starters, here are a few listservs that may be of interest initially. But remember, *Liszt* claims to list over 70,000 E-mail discussion groups.

part

1

- AMLIT-L American Literature
  Subscription Address: listproc@lists.missouri.edu
- ENVIRONMENT-L A general discussion of the environment
  Subscription Address: listproc@cornell.edu
- POETRY-W A general discussion of poetry writing
  Subscription Address: listserv@psuvm.psu.edu
- RHETORIC Rhetoric, social movements, persuasion
  Subscription Address: comserve@cios.llc.rpi.edu
- WHIRL Women's History in Rhetoric and Language
  Subscription Address: listserv@psuvm.psu.edu
- WRITERS The art, craft, and business of writing
  Subscription Address: listserv@mitvma.mit.edu
- WRITING A general discussion of writing
  Subscription Address: listserv@psuvm.psu.edu

Participating in Discussions

To participate in a mailing list discussion you must subscribe to or join the list. Each list has two addresses, the subscription or listserver address, and the submissions address. Use the listserver address to join or quit the list; use the submissions address to send a message to members of the mailing list.

Listserver addresses almost always start with "listserv," "listproc," or "majordomo."

For example, the list dedicated to writers of poetry is called POETRY-W and is managed by the listserver located at "listserv@psuvm.psu.edu." Submissions to the list are mailed to "POETRY-W @psuvm.psu.edu." Whenever you want to manage your subscription by joining or quitting the list, you send an E-mail message to the listserver. When you want to write a message that will be sent to the other subscribers of the list you send an E-mail message to the submission address.

Specific instructions for subscribing depend on how the list was set up, but the normal procedure to subscribe to a list is:

part
1

1. Send an E-mail message to the listserver by putting the listserver's address on the "To:" line of the message. Do not use the submission address for the list!

2. Leave the subject line of the message blank. If your E-mail program will not let you send a message with a blank subject, use "subscribe" on the subject line.

3. In the body of the message type "subscribe *listname*" where you will substitute the name of the list for *listname*.

In a short time you will receive E-mail telling you that your subscription request has been accepted, or you will get back an error message saying that the listserver did not understand your subscription request. If you get an error message the best thing to do is to send a one-line message to the listserver address that simply says "help." This will usually get you an E-mail message with all the details on how to subscribe to a list on that listserver.

Save the notice the listserver sends when you are finally enrolled as a subscriber. This notice will contain useful information such as how to get off the list, whether or not a digest form is available and how to receive it, how to get back issues, and so on.

After your subscription has been accepted the listserver will start forwarding to you, via E-mail, all messages submitted to the list. You can participate in the discussion by sending an E-mail message to the submission address. Remember that your message will be forwarded to many people, so follow the rules of netiquette.

If you subscribe to an active list, be sure to read your E-mail frequently. Some lists generate hundreds of messages a week, and your mailbox will fill up quickly if you don't log on frequently to clean it up. You may want to investigate the use of "mail filtering rules" or "inbox assistant" features of your mail reader program to automatically sort messages into folders as they arrive in your mailbox. Check the **Help** section of your mail program for the details of using these features.

The Internet as a Library: Using the Web for Research

part

1

The fastest and most popular part of the Internet is the World Wide Web. The Web consists of hundreds of thousands of computers, each publishing information you can use. Some of the information is very useful, such as on-line library card catalogs, information from organizations, and subject-specific information you can't find anywhere else. You'll also find loads of useless, tasteless, and incorrect information and propaganda. On the Web, everyone and anyone can be a publisher.

The Web got its name because each site usually contains *links* to other sites the publisher thinks are related. Since each site has links to other sites, a kind of web is formed. This is the great power of the Web. Once you find a site that contains information you find useful, you can follow the links to other sites you think may be interesting then continue with your research. This is like using the bibliography of one book to find other books, only much faster.

Structure of the Web: Making Order out of Chaos

Unfortunately, there's no overall organization for Web sites—no classification system or central catalog. Anyone can publish information on the Web. The result can be compared to a library without a book numbering system or card catalog. You must roam around until you happen to find what you are looking for.

The trick to finding information on the Web is to keep a short of list of sites that specialize in cataloging information from other Web sites, keep your own personal list of favorite Web sites, and learn to use at least one of the many *search engines* that will scan the Internet looking for Web sites that contain keywords or phrases that you specify.

Navigating the Web

Navigating the Web requires a program called a *browser*. The browser keeps track of where you are on the Web and displays the information sent to your computer by the Web site. Using the Web is an interactive process. Information is sent to you as you request it.

Information on the Web is independent of the type of computer you are using. It doesn't matter if you are using a Macintosh or PC-compatible. To view information on any site, all you need is a browser for your specific computer.

There are several browsers on the market, but the two most popular are Netscape Navigator and Microsoft Internet Explorer. We'll show examples from both of those browsers in this section.

All browsers offer similar basic functions. The basic functions are:

part

1

- Site Name Selection: Go to a specific Web site
- HyperText Link: Move to a new site when an on-screen link is selected
- **Back** button: Back up to the previous site
- **Forward** button: Move forward to return to the site you just moved back from
- **Home** button: Go to your home or starting page
- **Print** button: Print the current page
- **Refresh** button: Refresh the current display

Uniform Resource Locators (URLs) Each site on the Web has an address called a Uniform Resource Locator, or *URL*. The URL always starts with the letters "http://". The colon and two slash characters are required. These letters tell the Web browser that the address you are about to give is for a Web site. Next comes the name of the site itself. Most, but not all, Web sites use the letters "www" as the first part of their name. For example, Microsoft's Web site's address is "http://www.microsoft.com" and the Web site for the University of Illinois in Urbana-Champaign is at "http://www.uiuc.edu".

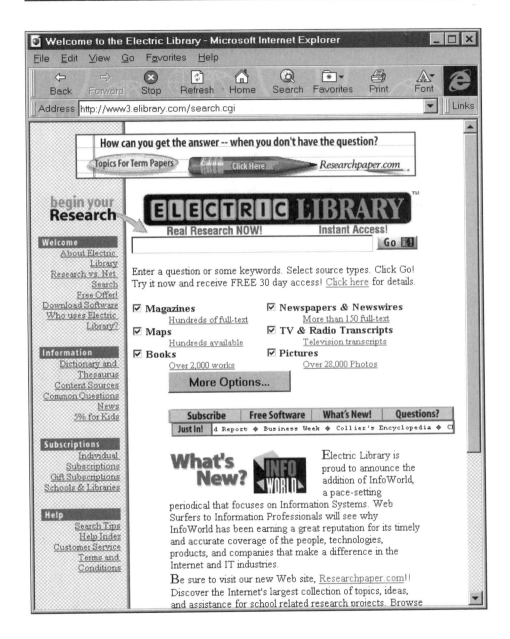

part

1

part
1

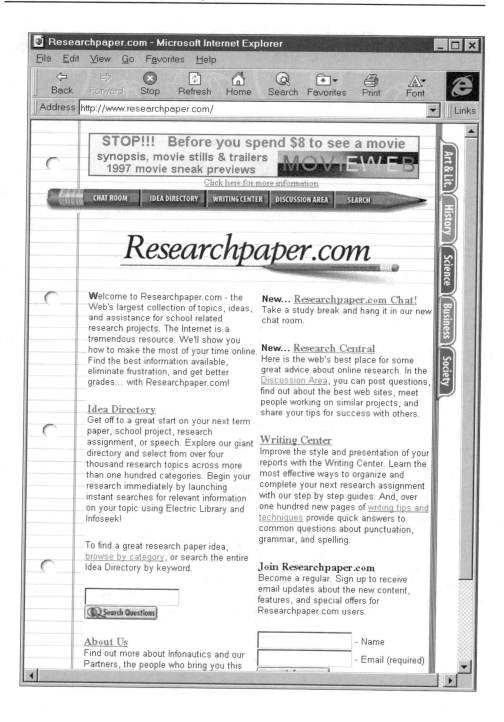

You can often guess the Web site address for large companies by typing "http://www.*name*.com", putting the company name or abbreviation in place of *name*.

The toolbar at the top of your browser window contains a place for you to type the address of the Web site you want to see. In Netscape Navigator it's labeled "Go to:" and in Microsoft Internet Explorer it's labeled "Address:". Both programs expect you to type the URL in exactly the same format. The URL for the site and page you are currently viewing will be displayed in this area as you navigate your way around the Web.

When you start your browser it will always take you to the same starting point or *home page*. The home page will usually contain links to other sites and so enables you to begin your Web exploration from a known point.

Browser Basics The actual display of information from a Web site depends on the computer you have, the browser you are using, and the features programmed into the Web page by the publisher. Some pages are only text; others are complex multimedia affairs that incorporate sound and video. Your browser will do its best to display the information from a site on your computer even if you do not have all the options required. For example, if your computer does not have sound capability, the browser will not try to play audio tracks from Web sites that incorporate them.

HyperText When you look at a page in the browser window you'll see some highlighted words and phrases. The highlight is usually a different color than the main text as well as an underline. Highlighted phrases are the *links* to other pages on the Web. Click your mouse on a highlighted phrase and the browser will jump you to the appropriate location. This type of text with embedded links to related details is called *hypertext*.

Some links are to programs or data files that can be downloaded to your computer. When you click on one of these links you will see a box asking for permission to download the file. Choose the "Save File" button on the dialog and the file will be sent to your computer.

Image Maps As the design of Web pages became more sophisticated, it was soon discovered that text links were inconvenient for many applications. For example, a site with weather information on the continental US would be easier to navigate if the user clicked a point on a map in-

part

1

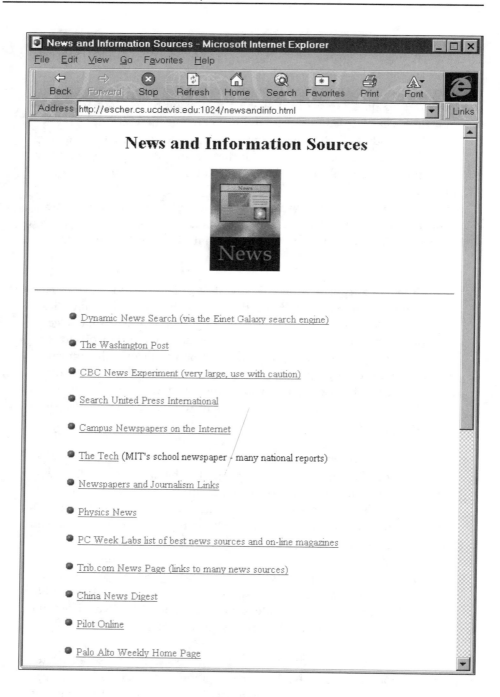

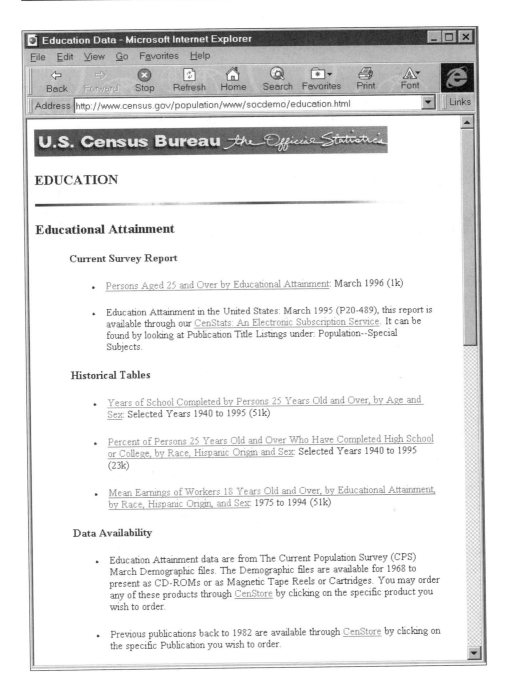

part

1

stead of choosing a location from a long list of text links. With this simple idea the *image map* was born.

Many sites incorporate image maps for quick navigation. You will see many uses of image maps as you navigate the Web. As you move your mouse cursor over a graphic, the pointer will change to indicate that the graphic is a clickable image map.

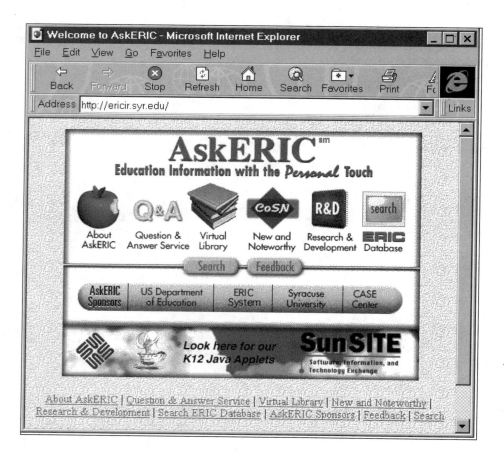

Using Bookmarks and History Files All browsers allow you to set electronic bookmarks, which enable you to return to a Web page without going through other links. This is useful when you find a site you think would be interesting to explore when you have more time, or when you finally find what you're looking for after following dozens of links.

Netscape Navigator files bookmarks under the **Bookmark** menu and Microsoft Internet Explorer files them in the **Favorites** menu, but they work the same way. When you reach a site you want to bookmark:

1. Select the **Add Bookmark** option from the **Bookmark** menu in Navigator, or the **Add to Favorites** option from the **Favorites** menu in Internet Explorer.

2. Navigator immediately adds the site name to the **Bookmark** menu. Internet Explorer pops up a window that allows you to edit the name of the site and to organize your bookmarked favorites in folders.

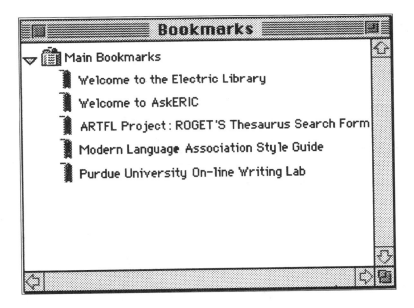

part

1

To return to a bookmarked site, pull down the **Bookmark** menu in Navigator or the **Favorites** menu in Internet Explorer and click on the name of the bookmark.

Your browser is also recording the name of every Web site you visit as you surf around the net. This is called a *history file* and lets you return to any site you have visited recently. Netscape Navigator gives you access to the history file from the **History** option in the **Window** menu. Microsoft Internet Explorer shows the history file via the **Open History Folder** option in the **Go** menu.

Customizing the Browser

You will find browsing the Web more convenient if you modify the browser to suite your personal taste and needs. The most common customizations are:

- Choosing fonts and colors
- Turning graphics, audio, and video on and off for faster browsing
- Choosing a start page

Netscape Navigator To customize Netscape Navigator, select **General Preferences** from the **Options** menu. The sections available include Appearance, Fonts, Colors, Images, Apps, Helpers, and Language.

Appearance
The appearance page allows you to make modifications by using fonts, color, and images.

part

1

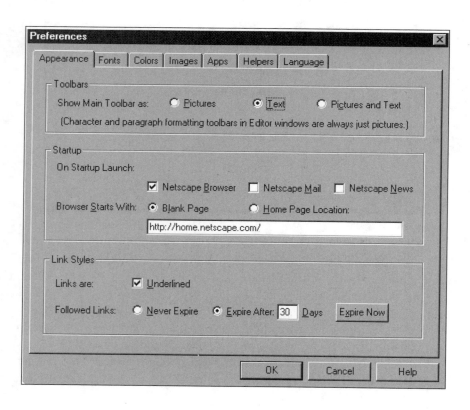

Toolbars Changes the way the toolbar in the main Netscape Navigator window is displayed. If you have a small monitor you may want to select "Text" style to reduce the space taken by the Toolbar.

Startup Specifies whether Netscape Navigator will show the Web browser, mail reader, or news reader when it first starts. You can also specify a Web page to act as a jumping-off point every time you start the browser. This is useful if you always want to begin with a search engine or the Web page from a specific organization.

Link Styles These options affect the way links are displayed and how long history files are kept. Leave these options at their default settings until you get more experience with Netscape Navigator. Then you can check the *Help* section for more detailed information on their use.

Fonts

The *Fonts* page lets you change the basic font Netscape Navigator uses to display the text on Web pages. There are two fonts you can set. The

part

1

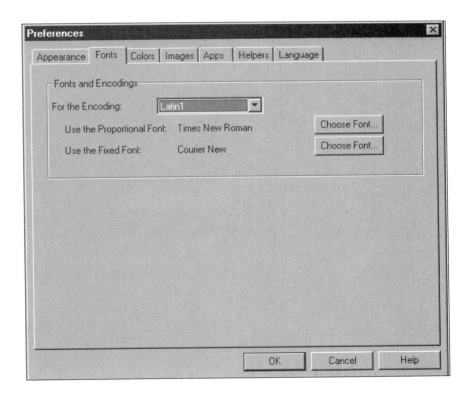

proportional font is used for all "normal" text. You may want to decrease the size of this font so the browser can show more of the page in the window, or you may prefer to increase the size of the font to make the pages easier to read. The fixed font is used for some tabular material, and does not have as great an effect on the readability of the display.

Do not change the *Encoding* selection unless you routinely visit non-English language sites and have a specific reason to make the change.

Colors

The Color settings are the default values used by Netscape Navigator if the Web publisher does not use specific colors. *Links* is the color of a link on the Web page. *Followed Links* is for links that point to sites you have seen recently. *Text* is the standard text color, and *Background* is the standard page background color. The default values are probably acceptable unless you discern certain colors better than others.

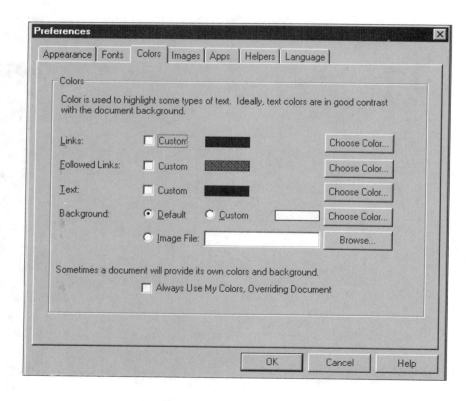

Images

This page lets you specify how Netscape Navigator will handle pictures displayed on Web pages. Leave the Color setting set to *Automatic*. If you have a modem on your computer and connect to the Web over a telephone line, you may find Web browsing faster if you change the *Display Images* selection to "After loading." This tells Netscape Navigator to load and display all text on the page, then the pictures. This setting can save you time. After reading some or all of the text while the graphics load, you may decide the site is not useful and go on to another without waiting for the pictures. Try the setting both ways to see which you like best.

part

1

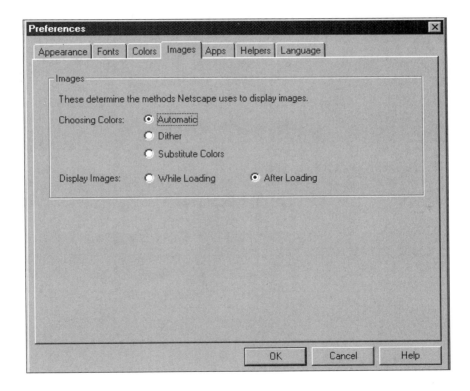

Apps, Helpers, and Language

Do not make any changes to the settings on the *Apps, Helpers,* or *Language* pages unless you have very specific reasons for doing so, and have the assistance of an experienced user.

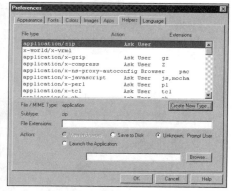

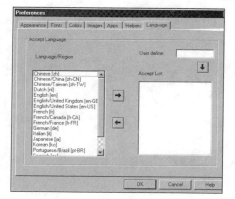

Microsoft Internet Explorer To customize the Microsoft Internet Explorer, select **Options** from the **View** menu. The option categories are listed on the "tabs" near the top of the screen: General, Connection, Navigation, Programs, Security, and Advanced.

General

The General options control the overall look of the browser.

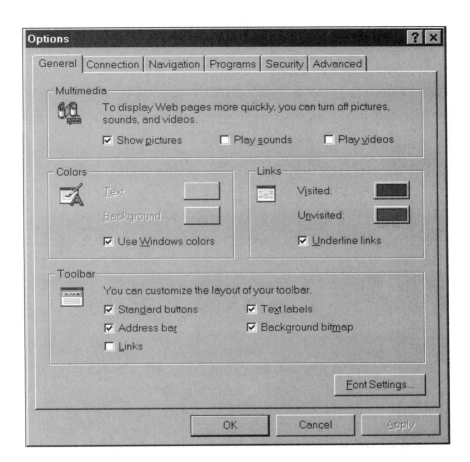

Multimedia Some Web pages include graphics, sound, and video: the **Multimedia** section controls which special effects Internet Explorer will download from the page. If you are connected to the Internet using a modem and telephone line, you can speed up the display of Web pages by turning *off* all three options. This is useful when you're surfing the Web and want to quickly scan pages. You won't have to wait for the multimedia effects to download to your computer; you will be able to move through pages much faster. When you find the page you're looking for, turn on the options you want.

Color, Links The **Colors** and **Links** controls allow you to customize the appearance of Web pages. These should normally be left at their default values.

Toolbar The **Toolbar** control lets you change the appearance and size of the toolbar. This is useful when you become an expert user and want to reduce the amount of screen space used by the toolbar.

Connection

Do not change the options on the **Connection** page unless you have specific instructions to do so. These options are set by the installer of the browser. If you make any changes here incorrectly, the browser will not work.

part

1

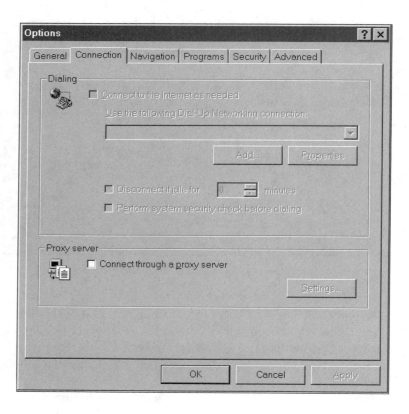

Navigation

The Navigation page allows you to change the Start page, Search page and links Toolbar page. You can also set the number of pages to record in the history file.

Customize The **Navigation** page lets you change the browser's "Start Page," the page that automatically displays each time the browser starts. This is useful if you always want to begin with a search engine or the Web page from a specific organization. You can also change this entry to the file "C:\WINDOWS\SYSTEM\BLANK.HTM" which is an empty page. This setting makes the browser start faster and is useful when you do not stay on the same page each time you start the browser.

History The **History** section controls the amount of space the browser will use to maintain your Web page viewing history. These options are normally left at their default values unless you are given specific instructions to change them.

Programs, Advanced, and Security Pages

Do not make changes to the settings on these pages unless you are given specific instructions.

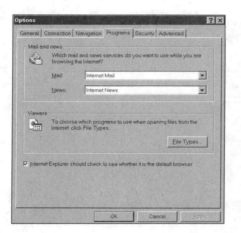

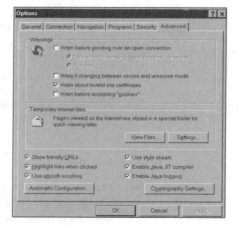

Searching for Information

When you start on a research project it's sometimes hard to know where to look for information. With so many diverse sites on the Web it would be impossible to visit them yourself looking for information. A whole new breed of programs called *search engines* will do the looking for you. A search engine looks through a giant index of Web pages which is created by robot programs that roam the Web collecting and indexing information. The index on the largest of the search sites, AltaVista (http://altavista.digital.com), contains information from 31 million pages on 476,000 Web sites. The search engine will look through this massive index for key words and phrases in a fraction of a second! AltaVista displays a link for any page that contains the words you specify anywhere on the page.

Another popular search engine is maintained by *Yahoo!* (http://www.yahoo.com), a company that maintains an index of Web sites. The *Yahoo!* search engine is based on categories and shows links to Web sites that cover topics you specify.

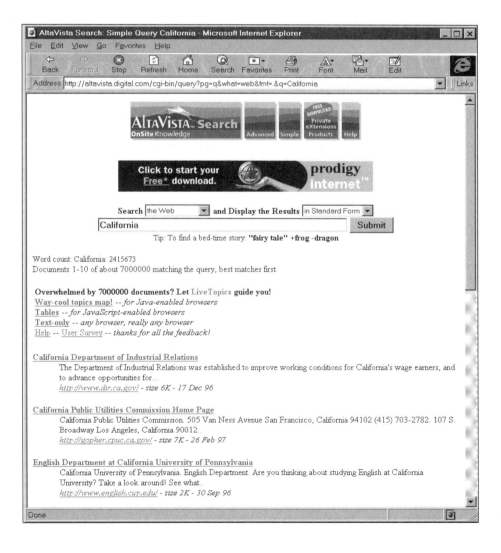

part

1

Using a Search Engine AltaVista indexes the contents of Web sites, *Yahoo!* organizes Web sites into categories. The difference in approach gives vastly different search results. *Yahoo!* returned a list of 105 categories and 5,210 sites that had the word "California" somewhere in their title or category name. AltaVista, on the other hand, found more than 7,000,000 pages of information that use the word "California" (there are probably a lot more, but it stops looking when it finds that many pages).

You should choose an index like *Yahoo!* when you are looking for sites that cover a specific category of information, like "finance." Use AltaVista when there is something very specific you are looking for, like "California deserts."

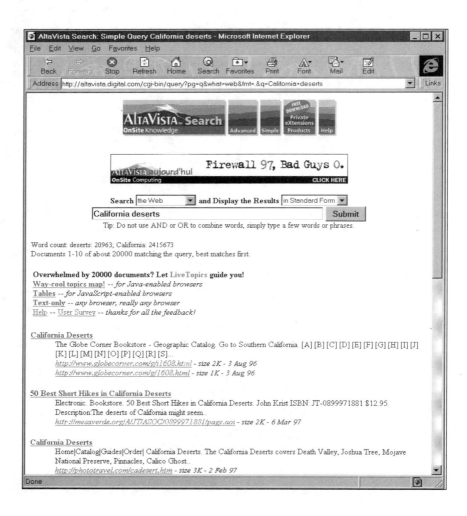

Simple Searches It pays to spend some time experimenting with searches and learning advanced search techniques. It's just as bad finding too much information as too little. Here's an experiment you can try with AltaVista:

1. Start your browser and point it to URL **http://altavista.digital.com.** (You should also set a bookmark for AltaVista so you can come back here without remembering this URL.)

2. To research a well-known movie, type **The Net** in the search box and click the Submit button. AltaVista will search its index for all Web pages that have the words "The" and "Net." The results of your search will be returned to you in a few seconds.

3. You'll see that "Net" was found more than 1,700,000 times and "The" occurred so frequently that it was ignored. Clearly this search is not usable.

4. Now type **"The Net"** as the search string and click Submit. The quotation marks are very important. They tie the words together so now AltaVista will only find sites that contain the entire phrase "The Net." This time about 30,000 sites are returned. That's still too many to be of any value. Very few of the pages containing the phrase "The Net," a very common phrase, actually refer to the movie of that name. You need to refine your phrase by narrowing it.

5. Type **movie "The Net"** and click Submit. The search actually returns more sites (about 100,000 this time), but this time AltaVista will organize them so the sites that have the most matching words appear first on the list. Chances are that if you were doing research on the movie you would find what you are looking for within the first few pages of links, or, if you had a specific aspect of the movie in mind, you could refine the search even further by adding more keywords.

part

1

The moral here is to be as specific as possible when using a massive index search engine and try to trim down the number of sites returned. You will also notice that the search engines try to sort the sites they find based on the relevance of the words you specify. Each search engine uses a complicated, proprietary formula to try to bring the sites that are most likely to be of interest to the top of the list. As you scroll down the list the links will be father and farther off-topic, and there's no need to continue looking. You're better off submitting another search with a slightly different set of words and phrases to see if you can find anything else.

Now use the URL "http://www.yahoo.com" to point your browser at *Yahoo!*.

1. Type **"The Net"** into the search box and click the Search option. *Yahoo!*'s classification scheme finds 21 categories that have these words and 3000 sites that have "The Net" in the title.

2. Type **"The Net" movie** and click**Search.** *Yahoo!* finds 1 category and 169 sites with these words in the title.

See what a difference the indexing technique makes? *Yahoo!* finds only a couple of sites that have relevant information because it's only looking at Web page titles. Because it searches entire documents, AltaVista is more likely to find what you're looking for than will *Yahoo!*. But AltaVista can also quickly lead to information overload.

Try searches in both sites and see which you like best. You can also try these other search engines, one of which may be more to your liking:

Excite	http://www.excite.com
Info Seek	http://www.infoseek.com
Lycos	http://www.lycos.com
Web Crawler	http://www.webcrawler.com

Avoiding Information Overload: Advanced Search Techniques

Some of the search engines offer an *advanced* or *custom* search mode which enables you to use special commands to narrow or widen a search. The most common special commands are:

AND

Use AND to narrow a search. This command causes the search engine to find Web pages that include all of the keywords you specify. For example, the search

"Chicago Hope" AND ER

will find Web pages that use both shows. A page that uses only one of these names will not be found by the search. The AND command is a great tool when you know exactly what you're looking for.

NEAR

The NEAR command is used to find any Web pages on which two words are "close" to each other. For example:

Shakespeare NEAR sonnet

will find Web pages that include phrases such as "Shakespeare's sonnets" and "the sonnets of William Shakespeare." Different search engines have different tolerances for "closeness," but the words you specify must usually be between 6 or 8 words of each other to be found by a NEAR search.

OR

OR is used to widen a search when you're not sure how to find what you're looking for. This command will locate all Web pages that include any of the keywords you specify. For example,

"Chicago Hope" OR ER

will find any Web page that mentions either or both of these shows. The OR command greatly increases the number of links returned by a search. so it's most often useful when you are starting a research project and want to get an idea of what's available.

part

1

NOT

Careful use of NOT can trim a search down when you know in advance that certain keywords should be eliminated. A search like

"endangered species" NOT plant

will find any Web page with the phrase "endangered species" on it as long as the word "plant" is not on the same page. w

These commands can also be combined. If you are going use the Web for research, it's a good investment of time to learn about these advanced search commands. Click the *Help* link in the search engine you like best to read about the various advanced searching features it offers.

Security on the Web

Avoiding Scam Artists and Credit Card Fraud Mail order catalog shopping has taken on new heights with on-line shopping via the Web. There are many on-line "storefronts" offering all types of merchandise and services for sale. Most of these operations are legitimate, but there are a few fly-by-night operators setting up Web sites. Use the same cautions you would use when shopping by mail or telephone.

- Know who you're dealing with. Be careful when dealing with companies or people you have never heard of.
- If a deal sounds too good to be true, it probably is.
- Be sure the company offers a money-back guarantee so you can return merchandise that you don't like.

There's a lot of publicity about credit card fraud on the Web, but it's not really much different than giving your credit card to a waiter in a restaurant. Someone at a store can write down your card number just as easily as the number can be recorded over the Web. The main rule is to know who you are dealing with and use some common sense. Be sure to check your credit card statements carefully if you start purchasing items over the Web.

Site Ratings Recent publicity and possible congressional action regarding the availability of pornographic and other explicit materials on the Web have resulted in a Web site rating system developed by the Recreational Software Advisory Council and enforced by the Microsoft Internet Explorer, version 3 and higher. This system, however, is totally voluntary on the part of the Web site operators, so it's by no means a foolproof system. If you want to restrict access to Web sites you find unacceptable or offensive, you should investigate the site rating system features of Internet Explorer by selecting **Options** from the **View** menu and then choosing the **Security** tag.

Virus Protection The Web offers many opportunities for you to download programs and files to your computer. Most of these programs are perfectly safe to download, but be careful when downloading programs from unknown sources. You may be exposing your computer to a harmful virus. Be especially careful if you download games or recreational programs. If you do a lot of downloading it's worth investing in virus protection software for your computer. A virus scanner looks at programs that you have downloaded and warns you if they contain viruses before the virus has a chance to infect and damage your computer's files.

Sharing Files with Others: FTP

FTP stands for File Transfer Protocol and is the means by which you copy files from someone's computer to yours over the Internet. There are many ways of transferring files, but the easiest one is to use your Web browser.

Both Netscape Navigator and Microsoft Internet Explorer utilize FTP in two ways. The first is by downloading a file when you click a link on a Web page. Links can be set up not only to take you from one page to another, but also to start a file transfer. The second way is to use the browser to browse to an FTP site instead of a Web site.

Retrieving Files from Web Pages

When you are looking at a Web page it's not possible to distinguish browsing links from file links, except by context. Click on an FTP link to activate it. The browser will display a message box asking if you would like to save the file on your computer's disk drive, or open the file.

part

1

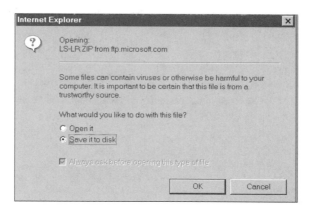

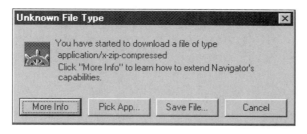

You normally choose to save the file. (If you choose to open the file instead, it will not be saved on your computer.) Choose the *Save* option and confirm the file name. After you confirm the file name a status indicator will appear on the screen.

Retrieving Files from FTP Sites

The URL for a Web site always starts with the letters "http://". For an FTP site the URL always starts with "ftp://". We're going to use Allyn & Bacon's FTP site as an example. The FTP address for Allyn & Bacon is "ftp://ftp.abacon.com". Type this address in your browser's **Go To:** or **Address:** window and press the Enter key. The contents of the FTP site will appear in the browser window.

Netscape Navigator Netscape Navigator shows the structure of the FTP site by indicating files with an icon that looks like a sheet of paper with a bent corner and directories with an icon that looks like a folder.

part
1

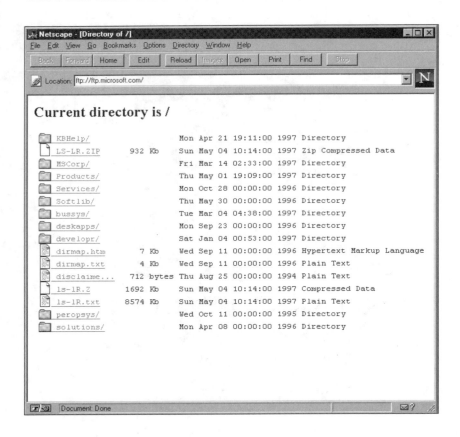

To download a file or see what's in a directory, click the highlighted link beside the icon. You will be asked if you want to save or open the file. Choose the *Save* option and the file will be sent to your computer.

Microsoft Internet Explorer   Microsoft Internet Explorer shows the structure of the FTP site by putting the size next to files and the word "DIRECTORY" next to directories. To download a file or see what's in a directory click the highlighted link. Choose the *Save* option when prompted, then confirm the file name and start the download.

The status indicator will show the progress of the download. If you are connecting to the Internet using a phone line and modem, a download may take a long time—possibly hours, especially if the file is more than a few hundred thousand bytes long. Be sure you don't need the phone for while!

part

1

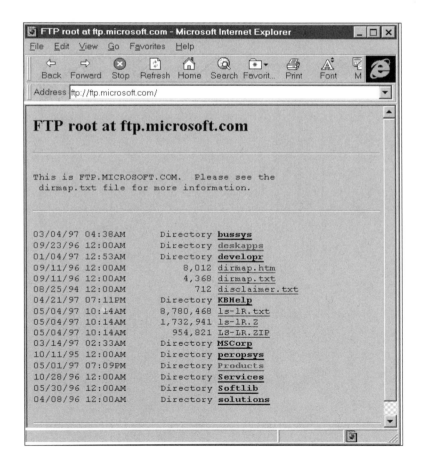

Posting Files You can make files available to other people by placing them on an FTP site. Each site has its own procedure for making files available, so you'll have to ask your Internet Service Provider how you can "upload" files to an FTP site so they will be available for other people.

part

1

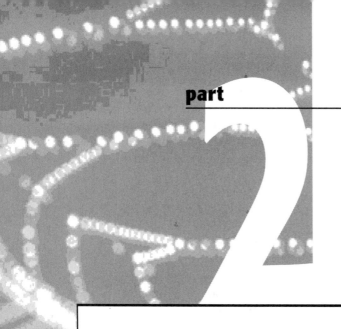

Information on the Internet

The Internet vs. Print Media

For centuries the printed book and later other forms of print media have ruled the storage and distribution of information, and those who controlled the media controlled the information and in some sense controlled the flow of information. "Controlled" may be too harsh a word here—not every author, publisher, editor, and encyclopedia-article writer has been obsessed with nefarious schemes to manipulate the minds of the people, and there have always been educators or other wise and informed people to warn of the danger of mindlessly believing everything you read. This attitude has, in recent years, come to be known as "critical thinking," learning to question what you see and hear and read before you decide whether or not to accept it.

For better or for worse (and it actually has been some of each), the print media and their built-in limitations have provided us with a filter for our information. Because publishing resources (paper, time, and effort necessary to write and carefully revise, readers, time to read) were relatively precious, only a small part of what humanity wanted to say could be printed. And somebody had to decide what. Presumably only the best, the most useful and valuable, the most interesting, the most worthy material was published, but every day there still was someone making decisions not to publish something.

There arose a special class of humanity: the writers. Some of us were writers; most of us were not. Authors, by their ability to compose and publish, had authority (the similarity of terms is not coincidental), had knowledge and wisdom, had permanence for their ideas.

However, today everyone is (or can be, leaving aside issues of access for certain groups of people for the moment) an author electronically. It is in some ways the embodiment of democracy—no one's voice is silenced. But in this new, cacophonous world, the sheer quantity and accessibility of the Internet have intensified the need for critical thinking. We are awash in a sea of information; in fact, some of what surrounds us can't even be dignified with the term "information." There is, for example, a Usenet newsgroup devoted specifically to the writing of unkind words about Barney the Dinosaur.

"Holy Wars" (i.e., arguments which are impossible to win, one way or the other, and which go on interminably) surround us and are, if anything, encouraged by the anonymity of the faceless conversations that occur over the Internet. We argue, in electronic print, about Islam vs. Judaism, pro-life vs. pro-choice, pro-environment vs. pro-jobs, about Macintosh vs. Windows, about purple dinosaurs; and, like the worst of the TV talk shows, the arguments often degenerate into name-calling, false accusations, irrational thinking and speaking, rumors transmitted as fact, and pure and simple lies. And this arguing and "flaming" can be broadcast to literally tens of millions of people.

The town lunatic who used to sit on his porch muttering racial or ethnic or sexual stereotypes was heard by almost no one and basically ignored or at least tolerated. Had he written a book or even a letter to the local newspaper, his words never would have seen type. Now, if he has a computer and a modem, he can publish to the world.

The challenge to the serious researcher becomes apparent: how do you judge what's valid and useful and what's not? Who can you believe, when everyone is shouting at you? What criteria can you use?

Critically Examining Your Sources

In many ways the problem of knowing what to do with the information you gather from the Internet is as knotty a problem as finding the information in the first place. You already have some experience with evaluating print media to draw on, however, so you simply need to be more

part

2

vigilant in applying your criteria since now there's no one—a publisher, an editor, a review board of knowledgeable people in the field—who is doing your evaluating and selecting for you. But the principles of critical thinking—whether applied to print media or visual media such as television or computer media—remain the same.

Critical Mindset

Critical thinking is, more than anything else, a habit of mind, a particular action you take almost reflexively when confronted with information. When using the Internet, it's crucial to question your information, to be a professional and committed Doubting Thomas. Assume, at the beginning, that anything you read is not true. Demand evidence or support from your sources. In the more interactive parts of the Internet—Usenet and listservs especially—you have the opportunity to question in person. In material you find that's not "live" and offers no interactivity, you must question your sources thoroughly, silently, and often alone. (By the way, never hesitate to try out an idea on a friend, a colleague, a roommate, or someone whose judgment you trust. That's just good writing advice and sound academic procedure.)

part

2

Try to imagine "what if . . . ?" or "what about . . . ?" scenarios, counterexamples that may disprove or at least call into question what you're reading. If someone writes, "It's acceptable to sacrifice the spotted owls because otherwise a lot of humans will be out of work and suffering," ask yourself, "But what if there weren't any spotted owls?" And vice versa. If someone writes, "Robber barons such as Andrew Carnegie are examples of the failure of capitalism," ask: "What about the tens of millions of dollars Carnegie gave to charities?" Make this kind of thinking automatic.

Probably the hardest part of critically examining a source or an idea is dealing with information you already know or already believe, or perhaps simply want to believe. If you're a lifelong Democrat, it's difficult to be critical of statements of Democratic principles. But it's just as crucial, maybe even more crucial, to do so. Your argument, your reasoning, your judgment, and ultimately your writing will be more convincing if you've examined and carefully critiqued your ideas, even your most deeply held ideas, and can show your readers that you've thought this problem through.

Repeat this mantra: Nothing on the Internet is true; nothing on the Internet is true; nothing on the Internet. . . .

Who Are You?

Part of evaluating your sources and your information is your sense of self, of who you are and how you want to appear in your research writing. If you want to appear calm, scientific, and detached, you will choose evidence that makes you look that way. If you want to appear more passionate and committed, choose that kind of evidence.

Specificity

One of the marks of a believable source is specificity—actual content, facts, figures, statistics, and research conducted or cited. If someone writes, "Most of the people who use the Internet are men," you may or may not be inclined to believe it, but you probably won't be swayed. But if someone writes, "Recent studies of Internet usage show that 78% are male, 90% are white, and 77% make over $60,000 per year," it sounds more convincing and can probably be verified by finding the "recent studies" referred to. But don't drop your critical guard—statistics can be misused, exaggerated, and even fabricated entirely (as these above are).

Audience

As in any writing project, you must know your audience well. You must consider what those who will be reading your research paper will accept as proof and authoritative commentary. If your audience will expect of you lots of facts and figures, then find facts and figures. If your audience disagrees strongly with you, you need strong and irrefutable evidence. If your audience is already on your side, you need more entertaining and enlightening data. If your audience consists of novices in the field about which you're writing, you need more accessible, easily visualized, and striking information. If your audience consists of other experts in the field, you need more precise and specialized information to make your case.

Knowledge of Speaker

How much do you know about the speaker/writer? Particularly in list-servs and Usenet newsgroups, it's possible to follow along for a few weeks and note who the frequent posters (a message sent to the list or newsgroup is called a "post") are and, more importantly, how authoritative they seem. Do they consistently know what they're talking about? Do other posters on the list recognize them as knowledgeable? Or does the poster have a history of flaming, of irrational and unjustifiable statements?

In Internet modes other than listservs and Usenet, it's more difficult to evaluate a source. Sometimes you can search in one of the engines for an author's or an organization's name and track done other works. This will allow you to get a fuller picture of the author, what she stands for, and what kind of biases or prejudices she seems to exhibit.

A Sense of the Writer's Authority

The writer's authority is not the same as what you know or can discover explicitly about the source: Instead it's a subjective feeling you have, based on the author's tone, grasp of the language, and conventions of the field. Most people can do this in face-to-face encounters—very often on meeting someone for the first time, you get an indefinable feeling about that person's knowledge. It takes a little more cultivation, but you can develop the same sense about someone's writing. If you have gut feelings about a source, trust those feelings until they are proven incorrect.

part

2

Verifiability

Much of what you read on the Internet will be unverifiable in the scientific sense of the word. You won't be able to reproduce experiments, find the ultimate source of information, or check out material presented as fact. In some instances, however, you will. Some information on the Net resembles pure academic discourse, complete with footnotes and a bibliography. Much material on the Net, however, ranges from flaming to carefully considered opinion.

Other Points of View

A critical thinker seeks other points of view like humans breathe oxygen. You need other viewpoints to help develop your own thinking, to learn by necessity how other people think and why they say what they say.

Fortunately, the Internet will often force an overwhelming multiplicity of views upon you, and in those cases where you seem to be receiving only one side of a story, it's a simple matter to find opposing points of view. When you are confronted with overwhelming amounts of information on practically any subject, both sides (or all twenty-five sides) will be represented somewhere.

In the narrowly-focused Usenet groups, you often won't find opposing viewpoints represented—that's the nature and purpose of newsgroups, to let people focus on a particular topic and discuss it. While posters to the newsgroup rec.music.bluenote.blues (a discussion group for blues music) may argue, for example, about whether Eric Clapton is or is not a great blues guitarist, you won't find anyone praising Bach. And if anyone did, it would be first of all a breach of "netiquette" (the largely unwritten code of social conduct on the Internet) and second, the poster would be driven off the newsgroup by either being flamed, humiliated, gently reminded that he's in the wrong group, or ignored.

Usenet and listserv postings follow "threads"—sequences of postings on the same topic, each one responding to the previous message or perhaps introducing a new perspective. This is the beauty of newsgroups and lists, and it makes critical thinking necessary. In fact, taken as a whole, a thread is critical thinking embodied. If you follow a thread over a period of a week or so (most don't last much longer than a week, burning out as participants move on to new discussions), you will be tossed to and fro intellectually as each new posting brings a new idea, a new perspective, a new "what if . . . ?" or "have you considered . . . ?"

In the less interactive modes of the Net (i.e., repositories of more or less unchanging information on FTP, Gopher, and Web sites), opposing points of view don't automatically appear. But you can search for them. You just need to remember to do so. Most Web search engines provide brief summaries of the contents of sites found while searching, so it's easy to tell at a glance when you've found conflicting information.

The following pages will give you practice in searching for, finding, and evaluating on-line information.

Critically Evaluating Usenet Postings

Usenet postings present the greatest challenge to your critical evaluation skills because of the amount of "noise" you have to filter through to get information. Usually, Usenet posters are just average people expressing their opinions—informed, misinformed; rational, biased; thoughtful, off-the-cuff. Occasionally there will be a posting by experts in a particular field who have substantial information to offer, but this is not as common as you would like it to be. Ultimately, recognizing misleading, inaccurate, or useless postings is a matter of skill, experience, and taste (different people will place more or less trust in the posting of an enthu-

part
2

siastic Rush Limbaugh supporter, for example), but here are some guide-lines that may help as you gain experience in the Usenet world:

1. Consider your first impulse if the posting you're reading appears to contradict what you believe, what you've seen and heard firsthand, or what most other posters in the group are saying. Start with your gut feeling.

2. What are the motivation, biases, and outright prejudices of the poster?

3. This is the hardest part: If you agree with the poster, or most other authorities you've read appear to agree, put yourself in the position of someone who disagrees with you. How would that person react to this particular posting? If you're prochoice and the poster makes an obviously prochoice statement, how would a prolife supporter respond (honestly!)? Recognize and critically examine the party line of *both* parties.

4. Try to verify with a second source any information you get from Usenet. How much of what a poster writes is verifiable fact, how much is well-considered opinion, and how much is just mindless ranting and raving?

5. Does the poster use inflammatory or blatantly prejudiced language? You know you wouldn't trust anyone, say, who refers to Italians as "wops"; how about terms like "FemiNazis" or "tree-huggers" or "Luddites"?

6. Who is the poster? What do you know about him or her? A poster who signs herself as an employee of the Environmental Protection Agency has at least a head start on authority and believability compared with one who signs himself a member of "Free Americans to Eliminate Government."

**part
2**

Beginning Questions for Discussion: WWW, Usenet, and Listserv Evaluation

1. Find an E-mail discussion list (listserv) that you might be interested in. Lurk for a week or two. Can you find its FAQ (Frequently Asked Questions)? How would you characterize the tone of most

of the postings? Are controversial issues tackled? Are there any flames? If so, for what reason? What seems to be a significant taboo on this list?

2. Do the same for a Usenet newsgroup. What are the differences between the newsgroup and the E-mail list?

3. If anyone seems particularly knowledgeable or authoritative on either the list or the newsgroup, after a couple of weeks send him or her a private E-mail asking for clarification or further expansion of some point he or she made. Do you get an answer? If so, how would you describe the answer?

4. In a thread from either the newsgroup or the listserv, try to find an example of:

   a. Flaming
   b. An unsupported assertion
   c. A misreading of someone's post
   d. An especially convincing argument
   e. An obviously biased poster

5. Find two different lists or newsgroups dealing with roughly the same topic. Contrast them: the tone, the willingness to either disagree or engage in verbal combat, the unwritten and unspoken assumptions behind the postings.

6. What is the difference between a search engine and a directory?

7. What are the parts of a URL? Give an example of a URL and explain what each part means.

8. What is a query?

9. Explain in your own words how the AND operator limits a category and the OR operator expands a category.

10. Is the search phrase "(coffee AND cream) OR sugar" the same as "coffee AND (cream or sugar)"? Why or why not?

11. Explain in your own words how search operators and other logical operators work in a query. Give an example of a complex query using both search and other logicals, and explain how it will be read by a search engine. What kinds of information do you expect it to find?

12. Use that query in your favorite search engine. Are there any surprises?

13. Enter a simple search with minimal search operators into WebCrawler. How many documents does it find? Enter the same search into AltaVista. How many documents does it find? How do the two searches contrast?

14. Begin keeping a personal chart of the strengths and weaknesses of each of the major search engines. Keep adding to it as you gain more experience with web searching.

15. Browse the *Yahoo!* directory (http://www.yahoo.com/). Find a general topic you think might be worth pursuing in a research paper; follow *Yahoo!*'s links to narrow that topic down and to find some initial sites where potentially useful information may be stored.

The Warmups

Let's begin warming up with some practice queries and search phrases.

part

2

1. Compose a search phrase that describes a group of desserts that are pies and that are either apple or peach.

_____

_____

_____

2. Compose a search phrase that describes a group of desserts that are pies of all kinds except cherry.

_____

_____

_____

3. Construct a query for AltaVista that will find, in the first ten hits, when Galileo was born. Try it; refine it if necessary.

_____

_____

_____

4. Construct a query for AltaVista that finds sites *opposed* to the Endangered Species Act.

_____

_____

_____

5. Try the query from question 4. What do you find? How can you refine your search to more closely focus on the goal?

_____

_____

_____

The Hunt (WWW)

part
2

In the early days of the Internet, there was a monthly contest called "The Internet Hunt," in which one of the few users of the Net would pose a problem for the other few users, and the first one to find the answer on the Internet (and provide documentation for how she did it) won. Once the Internet grew to hundreds of thousands and finally tens of millions of users, the contest became unwieldy and it was discontinued. But it was a good idea—many a budding Internet researcher cut her teeth on this contest.

So for practice, here is a list of new "Internet Hunts" on which to try out your new research skills. For each question, provide

1. The answer

2. The URL where you found the answer

3. The process you used (most likely, the query phrase and the search engine used, and perhaps the intermediate links you clicked on).

All of these questions will be answerable from the World Wide Web (or occasionally from its predecessors Gopher or FTP—all accessible via your Web browser). There will often be a variety of correct answers to parts 2 and 3—the Web is notorious for providing multiple paths to the same points.

Questions

1. Where is Karl Marx buried (city, country, cemetery)?

    Answer: _____

    _____

    URL: _____

    _____

    Process: _____

    _____

    _____

2. What is the name of the Greek astronomer who calculated the circumference of the Earth over 1,500 years before Columbus sailed?

    Answer: _____

    _____

    URL: _____

    _____

    Process: _____

    _____

    _____

part

2

3. According to Grant himself, what does the middle initial "S" stand for in "Ulysses S. Grant"? (Note: It's *not* "Simpson.")

    Answer: _____

    _____

    URL: _____

    _____

    Process: _____

    _____

    _____

4. How many blue whales are left on planet Earth?

Answer: _____

_____

URL: _____

_____

Process: _____

_____

_____

5. How many hours a day does the average American child watch television?

Answer: _____

_____

URL: _____

_____

Process: _____

_____

_____

6. What woman led the fight to clean up Love Canal in the 1970s?

Answer: _____

_____

URL: _____

_____

Process: _____

_____

_____

7. Who coined the term "rock and roll"?

Answer: _____

_____

URL: _____

_____

Process: _____

_____

_____

8. In what year did it become illegal for employers to discriminate against people with physical disabilities?

Answer: _____

_____

URL: _____

_____

Process: _____

_____

_____

9. Use the *Yahoo!* directories (*not* its Web-search function) for this one: What percentage of the population of Nepal is under the age of 18?

Answer: _____

_____

URL: _____

_____

Process: _____

_____

_____

part

2

10. How many times did Robert Frost win the Pulitzer Prize?

Answer: _____

_____

URL: _____

_____

Process: _____

_____

_____

For Discussion

Share the results in class with others.

- Did you all find the answers?
- If someone couldn't find one, why? What was he doing wrong?
- As a class, begin to formulate some helpful tips for finding Internet resources that seem to work for the whole class.
- How many *different* sites did your class find with the same answer to any particular question?
- And finally, did others in the class find different answers to the same question? (Many sites, for example, repeat without comment the incorrect information about Ulysses S. Grant's middle name being "Simpson"—would you have stopped after the first site that said this if you hadn't been told that it was incorrect?) How do you interpret the different answers to the same question?

A Closer Look at Hunting

part **2**

Now try this:

Use the same relatively complex search query in three or four different search engines (or as close to the same as the particular engine's rules allow).

The Query:

_____

_____

Run the searches on the same day. What do you find?

Engine _____

Number of Hits _____

URL of First (i.e., "most relevant") hit_____

_____

Engine _____

Number of Hits _____

URL of First (i.e., "most relevant") hit_____

_____

Engine _____

Number of Hits _____

URL of First (i.e., "most relevant") hit_____

_____

Engine _____

Number of Hits _____

URL of First (i.e., "most relevant") hit_____

_____

Citation Exercise
Write the "Works Cited" entry for one of the sites above in perfect MLA format.

_____

_____

_____

_____

part

2

Do the same one in perfect APA format.

_____

_____

_____

_____

For Discussion

■ There are very likely huge differences in the information found. What are they? How do you explain them?

■ Do any of the engines miss what appears to be an extremely relevant site that another (or most) of the engines found?

■ Can you draw any inferences about the relative strengths and weakness of each search engine? Is more always better? Is less always better?

■ Can you think of any situations where you would prefer one engine over another?

■ What do you wish the engines could do that they don't do?

The Critical Evaluation (WWW)

Now it's time to begin using your discovered information in your writing. You should keep in mind, however, that the Internet just exaggerates the problems of interpretation and evaluation of information. The problem has always been with us; it was just never so obvious. Printed information is capable of transmitting misinformation and biases; in fact, most rhetoricians today understand that all communication is the product of someone's interpretation. Finding The Truth is practically impossible. How can two separate juries look at videotapes of a group of police officers beating a man and come to exactly opposite conclusions (interpretations)? Even seeing, apparently, isn't believing.

You should try to engage the material you're finding in some intellectual way rather than simply looking for information to support your preconceived points. You're actually looking to expand your own ideas and range of knowledge. Examine the contexts of statements—try to understand the person behind and the motives of a Web site entitled "Rush Limbaugh is Right!" even if you can't stand Rush Limbaugh and his ideas.

Probably the single main difference between putting up a page on the World Wide Web and posting similar sentiments to a Usenet newsgroup is the relative difficulty of doing the Web page. You need either to know a special computer language called "html" or buy and learn special software. This added dimension of difficulty cuts down slightly on bizarre and freakish Web pages. The spontaneity of Usenet seems to engender more radical swings of emotion. But keep in mind, the thirty-nine people who committed suicide on a signal from 1997's Hale-Bopp Comet were all proficient Web designers, and their Heaven's Gate Web site is, at least to most people's mind, a model of careful, professionally made lunacy.

The listing of URLs in Appendix A includes a number of sites purporting to offer help on interpreting and evaluating Internet sources. But notice that they don't agree in all respects. So ultimately you'll have to integrate your ideas, your purposes in writing, your audience, and the information you discover into a rhetorically satisfying piece of writing.

Let's look at some of the characteristics of information from a Web site, not with an eye toward pigeonholing the information as either "biased" and therefore presumably useless, or "objective" and therefore presumably The Truth, but toward negotiating your (and your writing's) position in a world of gray areas.

Verifiability. This means that somewhere else someone has said essentially the same thing. In the sciences, for example, it means that the results of an experiment can be reproduced by anyone. If two people drop stones, both stones accelerate downward at the same rate. But in more humanistic areas, verifiability is not quite so convincing. Just because two or two hundred people interpret a certain passage in Shakespeare the same way or the upbringing of a future serial killer the same way, that doesn't mean that that particular interpretation is the most valuable, useful, or convincing.

Authority. Who is the author? If she's well known in her field and respected by her peers, then she's verifiably an authority, and her conclusions and communications will normally be more convincing to your readers. But not always. Authorities can be wrong, either accidentally or intentionally. And seemingly less authoritative writers can present interpretations that are more reasonable to your readers.

Author's tone. Is it strident or unreasonable, as if the person is trying to convince you by shouting louder, or as if the person is writing only for people who already agree with him and is unaware that other people will be reading it? Or does the writer show an awareness of his audience and try to situate himself within a larger culture by explaining his biases and noting how they may affect his conclusions? Biases aren't necessarily destructive of an author's tone, provided the author is aware of them.

part

2

Kind of information. Again, there are exceptions but usually more concrete information is believable. Normally countable things can be recounted by someone else (anyone else) and the answer will be the same: the number of cars sold in February, the number of fat grams in a Big Mac, the number of people abused by their spouses. But all communication has an edge or slant (does the count of "cars" include "pickup trucks" as well? Can you tell from the Web site?)

So, let's try some exercises to practice evaluating information found on Web sites.

Exercises

Using your favorite search engine, find a number of Web sites on a controversial issue. You may need to follow some links to get down to actual information and communication; many of the sites you find will simply be compilations of links on the subject. Choose four or five (i.e., specifically more than two!) that seem to take different approaches to the topic.

1. List the URLs and titles of your Web sites.

_____

_____

_____

_____

2. Which one is closest to your current view of the issue? Why?

_____

_____

_____

_____

3. Of the remaining sites, which one seems the most convincing? Why?

_____

_____

_____

_____

4. Which one seems least convincing? Why?

_____

_____

_____

_____

5. Can you determine who the authors of the pages are? Can you find out more information about them? (This may require a good deal of hunting! For starters, try searching on their names.)

_____

_____

_____

_____

part
2

6. Is any one of the authors particularly authoritative? Nonauthoritative? Why?

    _____

    _____

    _____

    _____

7. Which of the sites seems most inflammatory in tone? Point out some words or phrases meant to arouse a reader emotionally and short-circuit the mind.

    _____

    _____

    _____

    _____

part

2

8. Do any of the sites contain numbers, statistics, or other relatively concrete or seemingly factual information? Point out one apparent fact. Can you verify that fact in another independent source? Where? Can you find, perhaps, a source that contradicts or refutes that "fact"?

    _____

    _____

    _____

    _____

9. Which site do you find most opposed to your own point of view? (This should not necessarily be the same one you mentioned in question 4.) Can you understand, intellectually, why the author has drawn conclusions that differ from yours? (If the material is especially inflammatory, you may need to recast it in less emotional language to understand the author's reasoning.)

    _____

    _____

    _____

10. On the site you noted in question 2 (the one closest to your own point of view), can you determine weaknesses in the author's approach? Who wouldn't it convince? Why? How should it be recast to be more convincing?

_____

_____

_____

_____

_____

11. Can you envision changes you would make in any one of the sites (assume for the moment you have the technical expertise to do this!). What changes would you make? Why?

_____

_____

_____

_____

_____

part

2

For Discussion
Share your answers with the rest of your class.

■ How would *you* answer the same questions for a classmate's sites? (This works best if you can access the sites yourself.)

■ As a class, what do you find works especially well on a Web site?

■ How do the graphical images and other elements of page layout affect your reaction to the sites?

■ Do different people respond differently to the sites? How can you explain this? Is one person "right" and the other "wrong"? (If your answer is to throw up your hands in despair and say "everybody's entitled to their own opinion," is that *really* true or just a copout? Was Hitler "entitled" to his own opinion of Jews?)

■ As a class, try to establish your own guidelines for evaluating, criticizing, and using information from Web sites.

The Critical Evaluation (Usenet and Listservs)

The challenges for critically evaluating Usenet discussions are greater in some ways than those for Web sites. The ease with which you can fire off a hasty and poorly thought-out reply seems to increase the amount of static on the line. But this same ease means that experts and other people with valuable information and insights, often too busy to create a Web site, can participate in the free flow of a discussion and contribute significantly. There's more wheat and more chaff to be separated.

To begin, take a current event that seems to have inspired a good deal of media attention and perhaps even discussion among you, your friends, and your classes.

1. Using one of the Web sites that lists Usenet newsgroups, find at least two that deal with the issue. If none of them seems like an obvious candidate, search on DejaNews for the issue and see which newsgroups it appears on prominently. If possible, find a listserv or two that may also be discussing the issue. Subscribe to them. Begin following the discussions without at first replying or posting ("lurking").

   _____

   _____

   _____

   _____

   _____

2. Follow the threads. Is there any person (or perhaps more than one) who seems to post more frequently than others?

   _____

   _____

   _____

   _____

3. Find out as much as you can about that poster. What can you tell from the posts themselves? Does the poster identify herself with a reasonably descriptive signature? Use DejaNews to find other

part

2

posts, perhaps even to other groups, by this author. What do you conclude about her authoritativeness in this context?

_____

_____

_____

_____

_____

4. If you were going to reply to a post, what would you say? How would you say it? Can you think of other ways to say it that would be better or worse? For what reasons? Honestly, how do you think it would be responded to in the thread?

_____

_____

_____

_____

_____

5. Do any of the posters mention a numerical fact or other potentially verifiable bit of information? Does he tell where he found the information? Can you verify the fact independently? If not, do you accept it?

_____

_____

_____

_____

_____

6. Are any posters flaming another? Give examples.

_____

_____

_____

part

2

_____

_____

_____

7. Find a post that seems particularly inflammatory. Rewrite it in calmer language. What does that tell you about the poster's motivations and underlying reasoning?

_____

_____

_____

_____

_____

8. Can you find a "flame war" (a particularly nasty, personal, irrational exchange of name-calling and scurrilous allegations)? Why does it happen? How does it stop?

part
2

_____

_____

_____

_____

_____

9. Find an argument or position that you particularly agree with. Can you find weaknesses in the reasoning? Who would not be convinced by this reasoning, and how could you rewrite the post to make it more convincing?

_____

_____

_____

_____

_____

10. After the thread has progressed for a few days, how have other people responded to that same argument you noted in question 6? What objections or alternative interpretations have other posters brought up that you didn't foresee? What surprised you?

_____

_____

_____

_____

_____

11. Find a post that you tend to disagree with. What is the poster's reasoning? What merits are there to the argument?

_____

_____

_____

_____

_____

part

2

12. Do other posters agree with the argument you noted in question 8? What new reasoning or evidence do others bring to the discussion that may be additionally convincing? What surprised you here?

_____

_____

_____

_____

_____

13. Do any of the threads you're following branch off into tangents, sometimes even with new subject lines? What's the relationship of the tangent or "new" subject to the main thread?

_____

_____

_____

_____

_____

_____

14. Why does the thread end (they all do)? Boredom or lack of interest? Nothing left to say? The issue is resolved to everyone's satisfaction—a conclusion is reached? A tangent becomes more interesting? Why do you think no one responded to the last poster?

_____

_____

_____

_____

_____

_____

part
2

Citation Practice
Write a perfect MLA Works Cited entry for one of the posts from the threads you're following.

_____

_____

_____

_____

For Discussion
- How do Usenet and listserv postings differ from Web sites? Consider tone, authority, content, and verifiability.
- How are they the same?

- Could you tell when anyone other than a white male was posting? How could you tell? How was that person treated? Do treatments of women and minorities seem to vary from group to group, list to list?

- Pool your insights as a class: How did the reasoning, examples, and information differ from newsgroup to newsgroup? What slants or biases did you detect in the overall group? What do all the posters seem to take for granted? What assumptions *don't* they question?

- Do you sense that anybody's mind was changed, even slightly, over the course of a thread? How does this happen? Can you give examples from your own observations of your groups and lists? If no one's mind was changed, why do you think that happened?

- Characterize how knowledge is exchanged and worked out over the course of a thread. Could any writer *alone* have envisioned so many different angles to an issue?

- How do groups produce knowledge?

part

2

Resources for Internet Research: College Composition

Search Engines

AltaVista

`<http://altavista.digital.com/>`

Allows both simple and advanced searches of WWW and Usenet; fast and powerful.

Archie

`<http://archie.bunyip.com/archie.html>`

Searches anonymous FTP sites; latest version has added Web searching capability.

DejaNews

`<http://www.dejanews.com>`

Searches Usenet newsgroups.

Excite

`<http://www.excite.com/>`

An extensive multipurpose finder of information; includes a Web search engine, a directory, and other lookups; now allied with America Online.

Galaxy

`<http://galaxy.tradewave.com/>`

"Professional" Web search engine, along with Gopher and telnet searches and a directory.

HotBot

`<http://www.hotbot.com/>`

Powerful and customizable Web and Usenet search engine.

Infoseek

`<http://www.infoseek.com/>`

Allows searches of WWW, E-mail addresses, Usenet, and newswires. Also includes a directory.

Lycos

`<http://www.lycos.com/>`

Web search engine and more: directory, graphics, PeopleFind, StockFind, Maps, etc.

Magellan

`<http://www.mckinley.com/>`

A large collection of prereviewed sites (special "Green Light" database excludes all sites with adult content), along with a directory.

Open Text

`<http://index.opentext.net/>`

WWW searches; in Power Search mode, provides menus for Boolean search operators; simple to use.

Veronica

`<gopher://gopher.tc.umn.edu:70/11/Other Gopher and Information Servers/Veronica>`

Searches Gopher sites; full set of Boolean and logical operators.

W3 Search Engines

`<http://cuiwww.unige.ch/meta-index.html>`

A single page with access to most major search engines.

WebCrawler

`<http://www.webcrawler.com/>`

A quick and simple-to-use Web search engine and directory; now owned by Excite Inc.

Yahoo

`<http://www.yahoo.com/>`

Both a full-fledged WWW search engine and the most famous directory for browsing.

Fee-Based Research Services

Brainwave

`<http://www.n2kbrainwave.com/>`

Searches business and company information, copyrights, patents and trademarks, medicine, news, people and biographies, science and technology, social science, government and education.

Cognito

`<http://wwwqa.cognito.com/>`

A student-oriented information service with a flat monthly fee for unlimited access to documents.

Electric Library

`<http://www.elibrary.com/>`

Allows plain English searches of more than 150 full-text newspapers and 800 full-text magazines; free 30-day subscription.

Lexis-Nexis

`<http://www.lexisnexis.com>`

On-line legal, news, and business information services.

NlightN

`<http://www.nlightn.com/>`

Searches and retrieves from 300 databases of magazines and journals, books, reports, conference papers, the news, and Web sites.

UnCover

`<telnet://database.carl.org>`

A periodical index and document delivery (by fax) service

appendix

A

General Directories

Berkeley Digital Library

`<http://sunsite.berkeley.edu/cgi-bin/welcome.pl/>`

The on-line collection at the University of California; searchable.

Complete Reference to Usenet Newsgroups

`<http://www.tile.net/tile/news/index.html>`

A searchable listing of Usenet groups

ERIC Clearinghouse on Information and Technology

`<http://ericir.syr.edu/>`

The WWW starting point for the Educational Resources Clearinghouse.

Gopher Jewels

`<gopher://cwis.usc.edu:70/11/Other_Gophers_and_
Information_Resources/Gopher-Jewels>`

An extremely thorough directory of Gopher sites, arranged hierarchically.

Info Junkies Anonymous

<http://www.globaldialog.com/~morse/ija.htm>

A site for lovers of hard information, more pointed and less commercial than *Yahoo!*

Internet Public Library

<http://www.ipl.org>

A directory of Web information arranged like a public library.

InfoSurf: E-Journals and E-Zines

<http://www.library.ucsb.edu/mags/mags.html>

A categorically arranged list of magazines and journals available electronically.

LIBCAT

<http://www.metronet.lib.mn.us/lc/lc1.html>

Comprehensive guide to libraries (U.S. and worldwide) that have Internet presence.

appendix

A

Libweb: Library Servers via WWW

http://sunsite.Berkeley.EDU/Libweb/

Directory of on-line libraries in 62 countries; searchable by location or affiliation.

LISTSERV Lists Search

<http://tile.net/listserv/>

A searchable listing of E-mail discussion groups (listservs)

News and Information Services

<http://escher.cs.ucdavis.edu:1024/newsandinfo.html>

A directory of hard news sources available on the Web.

Social Science Information Gateway

`<http://sosig.esrc.bris.ac.uk>`

A comprehensive listing of social science information sources available electronically worldwide.

Supreme Court Decisions

`<http://www.law.cornell.edu/supct/>`

A searchable database of recent Supreme Court decisions.

Voice of the Shuttle: Web Page for Humanities Research

`<http://humanitas.ucsb.edu/>`

An amazingly comprehensive directory of humanities-oriented Web pages.

appendix

A

Webliography: A Guide to Internet Resources

`<http://www.lib.lsu.edu/weblio.html>`

A large, categorically arranged directory of Web sites, compiled by the Louisiana State University library.

WWW Virtual Library

`<http://www.w3.org/pub/DataSources/bySubject/Overview.ht ml>`

One of the first directories of Web sites, and still one of the most comprehensive.

Desktop References

Acronym and Abbreviation List

`<http://www.ucc.ie/info/net/acronyms/>`

Searchable list of acronyms; also reversible to search for acronym from a keyword.

The Alternative Dictionaries

`<http://www.notam.uio.no/~hcholm/altlang/>`

Dictionary of slang and expressions you most likely won't find in a normal dictionary; all entries are submitted by users.

CIA World Factbook

`<http://www.odci.gov/cia/publications/nsolo/wfb-all.htm>`

Every hard fact about every country in the world.

Computing Dictionary

`<http://wombat.doc.ic.ac.uk/>`

Dictionary of computing terms; often technical.

Hypertext Webster Interface

`<http://c.gp.cs.cmu.edu:5103/prog/webster>`

A searchable dictionary.

The King James Bible

`<http://etext.virginia.edu/kjv.browse.html>`

In addition to a searchable KJV, this site provides a side-by-side comparison of the King James and the Revised Standard versions.

The Holy Qur'an

`<http://www.utexas.edu/students/amso/quran_html/>`

Searchable and downloadable English translation.

Quotations Page

`<http://www.starlingtech.com/quotes/>`

Search for that quotation by keyword.

appendix

Roget's Thesaurus

`<http://humanities.uchicago.edu/forms_unrest/`
`ROGET.html>`

An on-line searchable version of the venerable book of synonyms.

Scholes Library Electronic Reference Desk

`<http://scholes.alfred.edu/Ref.html>`

An index of "ready reference" sources.

Shakespeare Glossary

`<http://english-server.hss.cmu.edu/langs/`
`shakespeare-glo ssary.txt>`

Alphabetically arranged text file of words from Shakespeare; not a concordance.

appendix

A Writing Help

Allyn and Bacon's CompSite

`<http://www.abacon.com/compsite/>`

An interactive meeting place for teachers and students to share resources and work on projects.

Anti-Pedantry Page: Singular "Their" in Jane Austen and Elsewhere

`<http://uts.cc.utexas.edu/~churchh/austheir.html>`

A compilation of famous writers who've ignored the singular "their" rule.

Capitalization

`<http://sti.larc.nasa.gov/html/Chapt4/`
`Chapt4_TOC.html>`

According to NASA's Handbook.

Critique Partner Connections

<http://www.geocities.com/TheTropics/8977/>

A place to find a writing partner for help by E-mail.

Dakota State University Online Writing Lab (OWL)

<http://www.dsu.edu/departments/liberal/cola/OWL/>

An on-line writing lab that provides writing help via E-mail.

DeVry Online Writing Support Center

<http://www.devry-phx.edu/lrnresrc/dowsc/>

Resources for integrating the Internet into your college composition classes.

An Elementary Grammar

<http://www.hiway.co.uk/~ei/intro.html>

Twenty-two sections of moderately technical discussions of grammatical topics from The English Institute.

appendix

A

Elements of Style

<http://www.cc.columbia.edu/acis/bartleby/strunk/>

Will Strunk's 1918 classic.

English Grammar FAQ As Posted to alt.usage.english

<http://www.lsa.umich.edu/ling/jlawler/aue/>

Answers to common grammar questions from linguist John Lawler.

A Glossary of Rhetorical Terms with Examples

<http://www.uky.edu/ArtsSciences/Classics/rhetoric.html>

Forty-five rhetorical terms (Alliteration to Zeugma) with links to classical text for examples.

Grammar and Style Notes

`<http://www.english.upenn.edu:80/~jlynch/`
`grammar.html>`

Alphabetically arranged guide to topics in grammar and style.

A Handbook of Terms for Discussing Poetry

`<http://www.cc.emory.edu/ENGLISH/classes/Handbook/`
`Handbook.html>`

Compiled by students at Emory University.

HyperGrammar

`<http://www.uottawa.ca/academic/arts/writcent/`
`hypergrammar/intro.html>`

Hypertext grammar course/handbook from the University of Ottawa.

appendix

A

Inklings

`<http://192.41.39.106/inklings/>`

A biweekly newsletter for writers on the Net.

The Internet Writer's Guideline Listing

`<http://wane5.scri.fsu.edu/~jtillman/DEV/ZDMS/`
`index.html>`

Guidelines on submitting to on-line publications.

The "It's" vs. "Its" page

`<http://www.rain.org/~gshapiro/its.html>`

The difference between the two homophones.

The King's English

`<http://www.columbia.edu/acis/bartleby/fowler/>`

Full text of H. W. Fowler's 1908 classic on English, Victorian style.

Nebraska Center for Writers

`<http://acm-www.creighton.edu/NCW/>`

On-line resource for writers of poetry, fiction, and creative nonfiction.

On-line English Grammar

`<http://www.edunet.com/english/grammar/>`

Especially suited for nonnative speakers of English; includes some sound files.

Online Writery

`<http://www.missouri.edu/~wleric/writery.html>`

"The conversation zone for writers"; tutors and writers meet on-line and discuss writing.

Paradigm: Online Writing Assistant

`<http://www.idbsu.edu/english/cguilfor/paradigm/>`

Almost a complete writing textbook on-line.

appendix
A

PEN Home

`<http://www.pen.org/>`

The home page of PEN, the professional association of writers and editors.

Poets and Writers Inc. Home Page

`<http://www.pw.org/>`

Support for professional writers and those who would be professional writers.

Politics and the English Language

`<gopher://dept.english.upenn.edu/00/Courses/Lynch3/orwell>`

Full text of George Orwell's plea for clarity in writing and thinking.

Punctuation

```
<http://sti.larc.nasa.gov/html/Chapt3/
Chapt3-TOC.html>
```

According to NASA.

The Rhetoric Page at SDSM&T

```
<http://www.sdsmt.edu/www/rhetoric/rhetoric.html>
```

Links to writing resources appropriate for both students and faculty.

University of Michigan OWL

```
<http://www.lsa.umich.edu/ecb/OWL/owl.html>
```

Receive advice about your writing via E-mail, link to other writing resources, or, if you're in Ann Arbor, make an appointment for a face-to-face tutoring session.

appendix

A

The Word Detective

```
<http://www.word-detective.com/>
```

On-line version of the newspaper column answering qustions about words.

Rensselaer Writing Center Handouts

```
<http://www.rpi.edu/dept/llc/writecenter/web/
handouts.html>
```

A collection of handouts on writing topics from "abstracts" to "writing with gender-fair language."

Undergraduate Writing Center

```
<http://www.utexas.edu/depts/uwc/public_html/>
```

Services restricted to University of Texas students and staff; links to resources for writers.

The University of Victoria's Hypertext Writer's Guide

`<http://webserver.maclab.comp.uvic.ca/writersguide/`
`welcome.html>`

Hypertext guides to writing and literature.

LEO: Literacy Education Online

`<http://leo.stcloud.msus.edu/>`

Help with "what's bothering you about your writing."

BGSU Online Writing Lab

`<gopher://gopher.bgsu.edu/11/Departments/write/>`

A Gopher site with downloadable grammar and writing tips.

English as a Second Language

`<http://www.lang.uiuc.edu/r-115/esl/>`

Bills itself as the starting point for learning English as a second language on-line. Includes visual and auditory resources, as well as a 24-hour help center.

appendix
A

Main Writing Guide

`<http://www.english.uiuc.edu/cws/wworkshop/`
`mainmenu.html>`

Three complete on-line handbooks for writing.

Non-Sexist Language

`<http://mickey.la.psu.edu/~chayton/eng202b/`
`nonsex.htm>`

Tips for avoiding sexist language, based on National Council of Teachers of English guidelines.

Purdue On-Line Writing Lab

<http://owl.english.purdue.edu/>

An extensive source of on-line help for writers, including professional help to specific questions by E-mail.

Researchpaper.com

<http://www.researchpaper.com/>

An impressive compendium of research paper help, including live chat rooms.

Scrivenery: Articles and Essays on Prose Style

<http://www.lit-arts.com/scriven/essays.htm>

An individual essay, plus links to resources of interest to writers.

appendix

A

Tips and Resources for Writers

<http://www.olywa.net/peregrine/index.html>

Materials for professional writers that are appropraite for beginners as well.

Word Wizard

<http://www.columbia.edu/acis/bartleby/fowler/>

A page devoted to the fascination with words; requires registration (free).

Writer's Center Home Page

<http://www.writers.org>

Resources for the creation and distribution of contemporary writing.

The Writer's Depot

<http://members.aol.com/WritersD/index.htm>

For a fee, professional writers and editors will critique your work.

Writer's Resources

`<http://www.vmedia.com/shannon/writing.html>`

Grammar, research, and general writing help.

Writers' Workshop: Online Resources for Writers

`<http://www.english.uiuc.edu/cws/wworkshop/writer.html>`

A directory of on-line writing help at the University of Illinois at Urbana-Champaign.

Writing Centers Online

`<http://www2.colgate.edu/diw/NWCAOWLS.html>`

A directory of writing centers nationwide who have on-line presences.

appendix

A

WWWScribe: Web Resources for Writers

`<http://www.wwwscribe.com/>`

Writing for the WWW, along with using the Internet as a research and communication tool.

Evaluating Information on the Internet

Checklist for Evaluating Web Sites

`<http://www.canisius.edu/canhp/canlib/webcrit.htm>`

Tips from the Canisius College Library.

Criteria for Evaluation of Internet Information Resources

`<http://www.vuw.ac.nz/dlis/courses/847/m2resev1.html>`

From an on-line Internet resources course from Victoria University, New Zealand.

Critically Analyzing Information

`<http://www.library.cornell.edu/okuref/research/`
`skill26.htm>`

Not specifically devoted to Internet information sources.

Evaluating Internet Information

`<http://milton.mse.jhu.edu:8001/research/education/`
`net.html>`

Specific guidance from Johns Hopkins University.

Evaluating Internet Research Sources

`<http://www.sccu.edu/faculty/R_Harris/evalu8it.htm>`

A comprehensive essay, not just a checklist.

appendix

A

Evaluating Internet Resources

`<http://www.mlb.ilstu.edu/subject/intrnt/`
`evaluate.htm>`

A worksheet from Illinois State University.

Evaluating Internet Resources

`<http://www.snymor.edu/~drewwe/workshop/evalint.htm>`

A checklist, links to more resources, and a bibliography.

Evaluating Quality on the Net

`<http://www.tiac.net/users/hope/findqual.html>`

An excellent and continually evolving paper from Hope Tillman, Babson College.

Internet Navigator–Evaluating Internet Information

`<http://sol.slcc.edu/lr/navigator/discovery/`
`eval.html>`

From Salt Lake Community College's on-line Internet resources course.

Internet Tutorial: Evaluating Internet Resources

```
<http://www.liunet.edu/cwis/cwp/library/internet/
evaluate.htm>
```

A short document from Long Island University.

Thinking Critically about World Wide Web Resources

```
<http://www.library.ucla.edu/libraries/college/
instruct/critical.htm>
```

A concise outline, from UCLA.

Web Site Analysis

```
<http://www.ccsn.nevada.edu/English/siteanal.html>
```

Focused on the issue of quality Web sites in general, not specifically on analysis of information.

Specialized Web Sites

Abortion and Reproductive Rights Internet Resources

```
<http://www.caral.org/abortion.html>
```

An extensive set of links to information both prochoice and prolife.

Alex: A Catalog of Electronic Texts on the Internet

```
<http://www.lib.ncsu.edu/staff/morgan/alex/
alex-index.ht ml>
```

A listing of full-length texts available on the Internet.

African Americana

```
<http://www.lib.lsu.edu/hum/african.html>
```

A moderately extensive directory of Web sites (and more) dealing with the African-American experience.

American Poetry Hyper-bibliography

`<http://www.hti.umich.edu/english/amverse/`
`hyperbib.html>`

A Web-based guide to American poetry, searchable on author or title.

American Studies Web

`<http://www.georgetown.edu/crossroads/asw/>`

A good jumping-off point for studies in Americana.

AstroWeb: Astronomy/Astrophysics on the Internet

`<http://www.cv.nrao.edu/fits/www/astronomy.html>`

An extensive directory of links and a searchable database of topics in astronomy.

The Business Communication World Wide Web Resource Center

`<http://idt.net/~reach/Lance/lance-cohen.html>`

A guide for business writing, with links to other on-line resources.

Digests of Education Statistics

`<gopher://gopher.ed.gov:10000/11/publications/`
`majorpub/digest/>`

Department of Education Gopher site containing statistics on education in the U.S.

Essays in History—University of Virginia

`<http://www.lib.virginia.edu/journals/EH/EH.html>`

Full text of the journal *Essays in History* since 1990.

FAQ: How to Find People's E-mail Addresses

`<http://www.cis.ohio-state.edu/hypertext/faq/`
`usenet/finding-addresses/faq.html>`

A guide to the often frustrating process of finding an E-mail address.

Fedworld Information Network

`<http://www.fedworld.gov/>`

The searchable gateway to the huge information resources of the federal government.

Feminist Activist Resources on the Net

`<http://www.igc.org/women/feminist.html>`

A compilation of useful links to feminist resources.

GPO Access Databases

`<http://www.access.gpo.gov/su_docs/aces/`
`aaces002.html>`

Another guide to government publications, on-line and print versions (with instructions for ordering print documents).

The Human-Languages Page

`<http://www.june29.com/HLP/>`

A huge compendium of links to resources in language.

Internet Movie Database

`<http://us.imdb.com/>`

A keyword-searchable database of everything you ever wanted to know about movies.

appendix

A

Journals

`<http://english-server.hss.cmu.edu/journals/>`

Alphabetical listing (with links) to hundreds of journals, both print-based and electronic, that have a Web presence; from Carnegie-Mellon's Humanities Server.

Library of Congress

`<http://lcweb.loc.gov/>`

The jumping-off point for the Library's on-line resources; not the whole Library itself, however.

Liszt

`<http://www.liszt.com>`

A searchable and browsable guide to listservs (E-mail discussion lists).

appendix

A

Media History Project

`<http://www.mediahistory.com/>`

A gateway to information on communications and media studies; searchable.

NASA Spacelink

`<http://spacelink.msfc.nasa.gov>`

NASA's fulfillment of its obligation to disseminate all the information it gathers through space exploration.

National Center for Health Statistics

`<http://www.cdc.gov/nchswww/nchshome.htm>`

The repository of the Centers for Disease Control's data.

The National Center on Addiction and Substance Abuse

`<http://www.casacolumbia.org/>`

The Web page of the think tank, devoted to providing resources on understanding the abuse of illegal substances.

National Organization for Women

`<http://now.org/now/home.html>`

A collection of on-site information and links to other Web sites for women's issues.

Nijenrode Business Webserver

`<http://www.nijenrode.nl/nbr/index.html>`

Searchable guide to on-line business resources, focused on the needs of students, faculty, and researchers.

On-Line Literary Resources

`<http://www.english.upenn.edu/~jlynch/Lit/>`

A searchable, categorized directory of academic sources of information in English and American literature; extensive.

appendix

A

Postmodern Culture

`<http://jefferson.village.virginia.edu/pmc/`
`contents.all. html>`

Current issue of the on-line journal of postmodernism.

Project Gutenberg

`<http://www.promo.net/pg/>`

The continuing project to make text versions of public domain classic literature available on-line; currently nearing 1,000 titles.

Religion

`<http://sunfly.ub.uni-freiburg.de/religion/>`

A starting point for studies in world religions.

Resources for Diversity

`<http://www.nova.edu/Inter-Links/diversity.html>`

A compilation of links to resources in issues of diversity.

Rhetoric and Composition

`<http://english-server.hss.cmu.edu/rhetoric/>`

An extensive guide to rhetoric, from the ancients to modern composition theory.

Science Hypermedia, Inc.

`<http://www.scimedia.com/>`

Focuses on chemistry, including an index of hundreds of full-text articles in the field.

Suicide Information & Education Center (SIEC)

`<http://www.siec.ca/>`

On-site resources, information, and links to more sites on issues of suicide prevention.

appendix

A

Thomas

`<http://Thomas.loc.gov/>`

A searchable database of all bills before the most recent sessions of the House of Representatives.

U.S. Civil War Center

`<http://www.cwc.lsu.edu/civlink.htm>`

An index of over 1,700 Civil War related Internet sites.

U.S. Senate

`<http://www.senate.gov/>`

A guide to business of the U.S. Senate.

United States Census Bureau Home Page

`<http://www.census.gov>`

A gold mine of statistics about the U.S. population

University of Virginia Electronic Text Library

<http://etext.lib.virginia.edu/uvaonline.html>

Provides access to the University of Virginia's extensive collection of digitized texts and images.

Voice of the Shuttle: Web Page for Humanities Research

<http://humanitas.ucsb.edu/>

An amazingly comprehensive directory of humanities-oriented Web pages.

Welfare and Families

<http://epn.org/idea/welfare.html>

The Electronic Policy Network's electronic journal, archives, and links.

White House

<http://www.whitehouse.gov/WH/Welcome.html>

The starting point for executive branch information.

appendix
A

World Intellectual Property Organization (WIPO)

<http://www.wipo.org/eng/index.htm>

A guide to resources on copyrights and patents in the electronic age.

 ## Current Events

CNN

<http://www.cnn.com/>

Multimedia, up-to-the-minute on-line news source; not adequately archived for searches.

Electronic Newsstand

`<http://www.enews.com/>`

An extensive listing of thousands of magazines; searchable, though most articles are not available on-line.

Forbes

`<http://www.forbes.com/>`

On-line version of *Forbes* magazine; searchable archives.

Fox News

`<http://www.foxnews.com/>`

News, business, health, sports, and technology.

appendix

A

The New York Times on the Web

`<http://www.nytimes.com/>`

The *New York Times* on the Web. Requires registration, but free.

The New York Times on the Web: Books

`<http://www.nytimes.com/books/>`

Web-based book section of the *Times*.

Newsstand

`<http://www.ecola.com/news/>`

Links to over 4,200 Web sites of print publications—newspapers, magazines, computer publications. Searchable by publication name.

San Francisco Chronicle

`<http://www.sfgate.com/cgi-bin/chronicle/`
`list-sections.cgi>`

On-line version; searchable.

Time Magazine

`<http://pathfinder.com/time/>`

An on-line version of *Time* magazine; search feature searches *Time* and many others; also provides access to bulletin boards and chats.

TotalNEWS

`<http://totalnews.com/>`

According to itself, "Information is the oxygen of the modern age. Total-NEWS is a directory of news sites designed to increase your access to information."

USA TODAY

`<http://www.usatoday.com/>`

On-line version of the national newspaper.

Washington Post

`<http://www.washingtonpost.com/>`

Online version of the *Washington Post*; searchable for past week.

appendix

Bibliographic Citation Guides

American Psychological Association (APA) Guide to Style

`<http://www.wilpaterson.edu/wpcpages/library/apa.htm>`

On-line version of the APA guide; abridged.

APA Publication Manual Crib Sheet

`<http://www.gasou.edu/psychweb/tipsheet/apacrib.htm>`

An intuitive and useful companion to the APA guide; may be more useful than the actual guide.

Citing Electronic Materials with the New MLA Guidelines

`<http://www-dept.usm.edu/~engdept/mla/rules.html>`

Modified MLA guidelines to apply to electronic sources.

Format for Citing Online Sources

`<http://www.cas.usf.edu/english/walker/mla.html>`

Janice Walker's page takes up where the MLA guide leaves off: on-line sources.

Modern Language Association (MLA) Guide to Style

`<http://www.wilpaterson.edu/wpcpages/library/mla.htm>`

On-line version of the MLA guide; abridged.

appendix

A

Web Extension to American Psychological Association Style

`<http://www.beadsland.com/weapas/>`

One proposal for extending the APA's guidelines to on-line sources; also includes a full set of links to the major issues involved in establishing the new standards.

World Wide Arts Resources

`<http://wwar.world-arts-resources.com/>`

A searchable gateway to the arts on-line, plus a directory of Web sites, chats, and bulletin boards.

Finding E-mail Addresses

Bigfoot

`<http://www.bigfoot.com>`

Supposedly the Internet's largest collection of E-mail addresses.

Four11

`<http://www.four11.com/>`

An extensive, searchable E-mail address directory, plus "yellow pages," a phone book, and government and celebrity addresses.

Internet Address Finder

`<http://www.iaf.net/>`

Claims to be the fastest E-mail search engine, with nearly six million addresses in its database.

Lycos EmailFind

`<http://www.lycos.com/emailfind.html>`

Associated with the Lycos Web search engine.

Phonebooke [*sic*]

`<http://www.phonebooke.com/>`

Searches *Yahoo!*, Usenet, and its own E-mail address database.

Switchboard

`<http://www.switchboard.com/>`

One of the most popular "people-finders" on the Internet; good for addresses and phone numbers, thin on E-mail addresses.

Usenet Addresses Database

`<http://usenet-addresses.mit.edu/>`

A list of the E-mail addresses of posters to Usenet (actually a huge number, when you think about it).

appendix

A

WhoWhere

`<http://www.whowhere.com/>`

One of the first, and still one of the most used, people-finders: E-mail addresses, phone numbers, home pages, business and government Web and E-mail addresses, 800 numbers, yellow pages, and more.

World E-mail Directory

`<http://www.worldemail.com/>`

Spreads itself thin, but your best chance at finding a non-U.S. address.

appendix

A

Documenting Sources from the Internet

In general, the rules for documenting Internet sources are the same as for other sources: Both MLA and APA use the in-text citation method. But there are some differences between on-line sources and print sources—lack of page numbers and lack of publication date, to name two examples. And information on the Net is subject to change—material is rewritten, moved, removed, duplicated, and linked. So, especially in the eyes of the MLA, it's important to note *when* you accessed a certain site. In the discussion that follows, only the special instances of citing on-line sources will be handled. For a complete guide to academic (print and other traditional sources) citation, use a good writing handbook or consult the MLA or APA guides directly.

MLA Style

This set of additions to the *MLA Handbook for Writers of Research Papers* was first designed by Janice Walker (http://www.cas.usf.edu/english/walker/mla.html), and later adapted into the *MLA Handbook,* 4th edition. In general, it applies the principles used by MLA to the special cases of on-line sources. Note that in-text citations remain the same as with regular print sources, i.e., author's last name in parentheses following the cited material.

WWW Sites (World Wide Web)

Author's name (reversed), the full title of the work in quotation marks, the title of the complete work if applicable in italics, the full http address, and the date of visit.

U.S. Fish and Wildlife Service. "Program Overview." *Endangered Species Home Page.* http://www.fws.gov/~r9endspp/programs.html (15 July 1996).

FTP Sites

Author's name (reversed), the title (which is not necessarily the same as the file name) of the paper (in quotation marks), and the full URL of the paper, i.e., address of the FTP site along with the full path to follow to find the file, and the date of access.

Deutsch, Peter. "archie-An Electronic Directory Service for the internet" ftp://ftp.sura.net/pub/archie/docs/whatis.archie (15 July 1996).

Gopher Sites

Author's name, the title of the paper in quotation marks, any print publication information, the Gopher URL, and the date of access.

Massachusetts Higher Education Coordinating Council. "Using Coordination and Collaboration to Address Change." gopher://gopher.mass.edu:170/00gopher_root%3A%5B_hecc %5D_plan (15 July 1996).

Telnet Sites

Author's name (if applicable), the title of the work in quotation marks, the title of the full work if applicable in italics, the complete URL, and the date of visit. Include other additional directions to access the particular file as necessary.

"Hubble Space Telescope Daily Report #1712." STINFO Bulletin Board (9 June 1996). telnet stinfo.hq.eso.org; login as "stinfo" (21 Sept. 1996).

appendix

B

E-mail, Listserv, and Usenet Citations

Author's name (if known), the subject in quotation marks, the address of the listserv or newsgroup, and the date of the posting.

Liberty Northwest. "Who funds the greenies." alt.politics.libertarian (15 July 1996).

Schultz, Joan. "Re: Halley's Comet." Personal E-mail (15 Jan. 1996).

MOOs, MUDs, IRC, etc.

The name of the speaker(s) and type of communication (i.e., Personal Interview or MOO posting), the address if applicable, and the date in parentheses.

Guest. Personal Interview. telnet du.edu 8888 (18 August 1996).

APA Style

The *Publication Manual of the American Psychological Association* (4th ed.) is fairly dated in its handling of on-line sources, having been published before the rise of the WWW and the generally recognized format for URLs. The format that follows is based on the APA manual, with modifications proposed by Russ Dewey (http://www.gasou.edu/ psychweb/tipsheet/apacrib.htm). It's important to remember that, unlike the MLA, the APA does not include temporary or transient sources (e.g., letters, phone calls, etc.) in its "References" page, preferring to handle them in in-text citations exclusively. This rule holds for electronic sources as well: E-mail, MOOs/MUDs, listserv postings, etc., are not included in the "References" page, merely cited in text, e.g., "But Wilson has rescinded his earlier support for these policies" (Charles Wilson, personal E-mail to the author, 20 November 1996). But also note that many listservs and Usenet groups and MOOs actually archive their correspondences, so that there is a permanent site (usually a Gopher or FTP server) where those documents reside. In that case, you would want to find the archive and cite it as an unchanging source. Strictly speaking, according to the APA manual, a file from an FTP site should be referenced as follows:

Deutsch, P. (1991). "archie-An electronic directory service for the Internet" [On-line]. Available FTP: ftp.sura.net Directory: pub/archie/docs File: whatis.archie.

However, the increasing familiarity of Net users with the convention of a URL makes the prose description of how to find a file ("Available FTP: ftp.sura.net Directory: pub/archie/docs File: whatis.archie") unnecessary. Simply specifying the URL should be enough.

So, with such a modification of the APA format, citations from the standard Internet sources would appear as follow:

FTP Site

Deutsch, P. (1991) "Archie-An electronic directory service for the Internet." [On-line]. Available: ftp://ftp.sura.net/pub/archie/docs/whatis.archie.

Gopher Site

Massachusetts Higher Education Coordinating Council. (1994) [On-line]. Using coordination and collaboration to address change. Available: gopher://gopher.mass.edu:170/00gopher_root%3A%5B_hecc%5D_plan.

World Wide Web Page:

U.S. Fish and Wildlife Service. (1996) Program overview. [On-line]. Available: http://www.fws.gov/~r9endspp/programs.html.

appendix

B

Glossary

browser
The computer program that lets you view the contents of Web sites.

cross post
Simultaneously send a message to more than one *newsgroup*.

digest
A compilation of several messages posted to an Internet *newsgroup*, sent to subscribers as a single message.

download
Copying a file from another computer to your computer over the Internet.

emoticon
A number of characters (usually punctuation) typed together to make a picture. For example, a smiley face is written as the emoticon shown below.

:-)

E-mail
Electronic mail.

FAQ
Frequently Asked Questions.

flame

A rude or derogatory message directed as a personal attack against an individual or group.

flame war

An exchange of flames (see above).

home page

A page on the World Wide Web that acts as a starting point for information about a person or organization.

hypertext

Text that contains embedded *links* to other pages of text. Hypertext enables the reader to navigate between pages of related information by following links in the text.

link

A reference to a location on the Web that is embedded in the text of Web page. Links are usually highlighted with a different color or underline to make them easily visible.

list

A mechanism for automatically sending *E-mail* messages to a group of subscribers.

listserver

A computer program that manages a *list*.

lurker

A passive reader of an Internet *newsgroup*. A lurker reads messages, but does not participate in the discussion by posting or responding to messages.

newbie

A new user of the Internet.

newsgroup

A discussion forum in which all participants can read all messages and public replies between the participants.

post
When used as a verb, "post" means to send a message. When used as a noun, "post" is a synonym for "message."

search engine
A computer program that will locate Web sites or files based on specified criterion.

spam
Spam is to the Internet as unsolicited junk mail is to the postal system.

thread
A series of messages in which a discussion is carried out.

URL
Uniform Resource Locator: The notation for specifying Web page addresses (e.g., http://www.aba con.com).

Usenet
The section of the Internet that is devoted to *newsgroups*.